WHEN THE GLOVES COME OFF

WHY AMERICA'S FAMILIES ARE FIGHTING EACH OTHER IN COURT

SALLY D. BABBITT, JD

Post-Graduate Certificate in Forensic Psychology, SDSU

ISBN 978-1-66782-582-3 (Print)
ISBN 978-1-66782-583-0 (eBook)

This book is dedicated to my husband, kids, grandchildren, and colleagues who believed in me when I didn't believe in myself.

Your advice, encouragement, and support have been the wind beneath my wings. And if you don't think I'm listening, note that there is no Dominick Chalupa in this book because, of course, a Chalupa is a food item.

Love and hugs, Sally/Mom/Grammy Sally

TABLE OF CONTENTS

INTRODUCTION

I always think of myself as the "accidental attorney" because I never really had a desire to become a lawyer. After a 10-year career in corporate accounting I chose to stay home and raise my kids and honestly didn't think I would ever return to the workforce full time. But I'm a lifelong student at heart and decided, "Hey, we have a law school 10 minutes down the road with flexible scheduling, why not get a law degree? That would be interesting." So I chipped away at my degree modifying my class schedule as my kids' schedules changed until I finally graduated and passed the bar exam. But the unexpected demise of a 20-year marriage forced me to return to the workforce full time with two teenagers at home. Luckily I had the law degree in hand.

I had no idea what area of law I wanted to practice in because, again, I didn't really think I would be doing it full time. But with my accounting background and family business experience, I had working knowledge of estate planning—wills and trusts and succession planning for families. It seemed a natural transition into practicing law. But going to court? Ummm, no. That terrified me.

So I stayed within my comfort zone by limiting my practice to transactional law (document review and drafting such as wills, trusts, real estate transactions, etc.) until I had an opportunity to take over a local attorney's thriving law practice when she became a judge. And with that law practice, I inherited a trial practice as well. It became baptism by fire.

Because the practice was in a small town, I had to learn and practice in many different types of law. For some reason I was hired to do more than a couple of lawsuits in the probate court. I didn't realize it at the time, but that is called "probate litigation." Not only did I find them interesting and something I could get excited about, but I discovered that I was pretty good at them! There was something about them that I "got." In fact, one of my cases went up to the Michigan Court of Appeals twice and the court affirmed my victory in the trial court! And I loved to dig deeper to find out what was really behind the lawsuit (spoiler alert—family dysfunction). I spent a lot of time doing research (not billing for it) and learning on the fly about trial skills, and I was extremely lucky to have a judge who either had tremendous empathy towards me or wanted to mentor me as well as he could. I will be forever grateful to the Honorable Michael Skinner, Eaton County Probate Judge, who valiantly battled cancer from the day he took the bench through his last breath. You are my hero.

After a period of time, I began to limit my practice to issues related to death and incapacity. Either on the planning side of consulting with clients and preparing wills and trusts and other estate planning documents for them, or in representing them in contested probate matters. During the pandemic of 2020, I returned to school via the world wide web and earned a post-graduate certificate in forensic psychology. That's when the idea for this book was born. At last I could use my combined knowledge and experience in probate litigation and forensic psychology to unmask the circumstances that drive families into battle via the courts. I have enjoyed writing and developing this book and I hope you find it interesting, educational, and often times amusing. Because as they say, "You can't make this *%#& up."

Initially this book was intended to be a book for attorneys who either already practice probate litigation or are thinking of practicing probate litigation. It was designed with the goal of giving the practitioner some additional insight into what is really behind these cases so that they could better serve their clients and resolve the family disputes. However, as I continued to read through my notes and drafts and talked to people about the book I realized that this was some interesting stuff! So the final version of this book is for anyone who is interested in avoiding a family dispute in court, is currently or has been previously involved in a family dispute in court either as an attorney or a party, or just plain has an interest in how this stuff happens.

The book is organized into six chapters. One chapter focuses on the legal authority and procedural aspects of probate litigation, which I think is essential to anyone understanding what is really going on these matters. One chapter focuses on what it's like to be the lawyer on these matters—it's probably not what you think it is. The remaining chapters discuss the situational and psychological reasons that I have found to be root causes of these lawsuits and family dysfunctions.

I look forward to hearing from you readers as to which chapters you liked the best and what, if anything, you may have learned from this book. Enjoy!

CHAPTER 1:

WHAT IS PROBATE LITIGATION AND WHY WRITE THIS BOOK?

I. What is Probate Litigation?

As an initial note, I solely refer to Michigan law because that is where I am licensed and I do not make any claims as to how other jurisdictions handle these cases as it would be outside my area of expertise and outside the scope of this book to do so. Probate litigation refers to contested/litigated cases under the jurisdiction of the probate court. These matters tend to revolve around challenging the validity of a will, trust, power of attorney, or some other legal document; challenging whether a person needs a guardian ("GA") or conservator ("CA"); or challenging the reports or acts of a fiduciary (personal representative ["PR"], trustee, agent under DPOA, etc.). In essence, these are family feuds.

Probate litigation differs in many respects from general civil litigation, personal injury, domestic relations, and criminal cases.

To begin with, the parties to the case are typically related to one another—family members. This is different than most other cases because civil cases tend to involve a plaintiff versus an insurance company, and criminal cases involve the state versus a criminal, or sometimes civil cases involve people who know each other but aren't related, such as neighbors or business associates. In domestic relations cases, such as divorce, custody, or parental rights cases, the parties typically start out related, as in a divorce case, and they clearly have had a significant personal relationship with each other. However, once the assets have been divided between the parties, the only other ongoing issues are between parents disputing parenting time or how much money one may be paying to the other in support. They are unique from most other types of cases, but they are also unique from probate cases.

For example, in probate litigation, individuals don't necessarily have to be an active part of the lawsuit in order to be involved. In probate litigation, individuals are considered to be "interested parties" if they fall under one of the categories in the four pages of the Michigan Court Rule ("MCR") MCR 5.125. Being an interested party ("IP") to litigation means that the person is entitled to copies and notices regarding all court filings, all discovery events (depositions), and all court events (hearings). They may decide that they want nothing to do with the lawsuit, but they will still receive all notifications throughout the case. And if the case gets resolved between the main parties, the interested parties must also sign off on the agreement even if they haven't been a part of the litigation. Again, this is unique to the probate litigation process.

Another unique feature of probate litigation is that the MCRs contain an entire chapter of rules addressing probate proceedings. The rules in Chapter 5 are limited, but they prevail over the rules in the general court rules where they exist. For example, in probate courts, the pleadings are called "applications or petitions" unless you are bringing a civil suit in probate court, then you use a "summons and complaint." In many ways, the probate court still functions as a court of equity. It's also been called the "Court of Compassion" because it helps individuals get court assistance with minors, elderly, and incapacitated individuals.

In a will or trust contest, typically an adult child is omitted from the will or trust and they challenge the validity of the document based on a lack of testamentary capacity or based on undue influence over the decedent by someone who benefitted more than the challenger. Lack of testamentary capacity can be difficult to prove, however. Often the medical records of the decedent are difficult to obtain due to HIPAA regulations or the records do not include any smoking gun diagnoses of incapacity. In addition, capacity is a moving target. In particular, dementia patients tend to suffer cognitive decline over a period of time, and in various areas of the brain. Therefore, on any given day, or at any given hour for that matter, their cognitive abilities and mental capacity may swing from very functional to total confusion or memory loss. And the determining time of capacity is the time that the document was signed.

In Michigan, where the Estates and Protected Individuals Code ("EPIC") is the controlling statute for testamentary capacity, the standard for having testamentary capacity is

MCL 700.2501: (1) An individual 18 years of age or older who has sufficient mental capacity may make a will.

(2) An individual has sufficient mental capacity to make a will if all of the following requirements are met:

(a) The individual has the ability to understand that he or she is providing for the disposition of his or her property after death.

(b) The individual has the ability to know the nature and extent of his or her property.

(c) The individual knows the natural objects of his or her bounty.

(d) The individual has the ability to understand in a reasonable manner the general nature and effect of his or her act in signing the will.

Essentially, if they know who they are, who their children/ family members are, and a general idea of their assets, and they understand that by signing the will they are providing for the distribution of those assets upon their death, they pass the test.

Fortunately, the drafters of the Estates and Protected Individuals Code Michigan Trust Code ("MTC") made it easy to determine the requisite capacity for creating a revocable trust in MCL 700.7601: "The capacity required to create, amend, revoke, or add property to a revocable trust, or to direct the actions of the trustee of a revocable trust, is the same as that required to make a will."

In order to prove a lack of capacity, the challenger must almost always have the testimony of the drafting attorney of the document and witnesses of the signing of the document by the decedent, to the extent possible. It's difficult to find witnesses who will admit that the decedent didn't understand what they were signing, especially the drafting attorney, since this would undoubtedly lead to a malpractice suit being filed against them.

The other avenue for challenging the validity of a will or trust is to prove that the document was signed as a result of undue influence over the decedent. Again, this determination is made based on the time of the document signing and it's hard to find witnesses and attorneys who will support the claim. Undue influence is a more complicated and difficult claim to support. Although it seems easier to prove than something as documented as a person's cognitive capacity, particularly in the elderly, it's actually much more challenging to prevail on.

Undue influence is a result of threats, misrepresentation, undue flattery, fraud, or physical or moral coercion *sufficient to overpower volition, destroy free agency, and impel the person to act against the person's inclination and free will.* At first blush this sounds easy to prove. However, there are often indicators of undue influence, but no actual undue influence occurs, or if it does, it's virtually impossible to prove in court. Indicators that often cause a family member to be suspicious of undue influence include the decedent placing significant trust in another person (often an unlikely person such as a caregiver); isolation of the decedent from family, friends, or other people who may pick up clues of a bad situation; some type of vulnerability of the decedent such as advanced age, limited mobility, cognitive decline, etc.; and few or no outside advisors such as an accountant, lawyer, or investment advisor (although I have been involved in a case where the investment advisor was the individual accused of exercising undue influence).

Certain situations will lend themselves to undue influence as well, including the recent death of a spouse or child, a lack of family members or nearby family members, dysfunctional family dynamics, living alone or with the influencer, fear of being moved to a care facility, use of multiple medications, and other situations that make a person vulnerable to exploitation. These situations make proving specific acts of undue influence even harder to prove because there typically isn't anyone around to witness the threats, misrepresentations, and influence.

Of course, the undue influence must result in some type of financial gain by the influencer. Sometimes that's in the form of a new or updated will or trust, or by adding the influencer to bank accounts or as beneficiaries, or even by the influencer being paid for "caregiving services" or other household services with or without the decedent's knowledge and far in excess of what the open market would bear.

In certain situations, there is a presumption of undue influence. This occurs when "[t]he person claiming that undue influence occurred has the burden of proving the following:

1. a confidential or fiduciary relationship exists,

2. the alleged perpetrator benefits from a transaction, and

3. the alleged perpetrator had the opportunity to influence the alleged victim in making the transaction." *(In re Erickson Estate, 202 Mich App 329, 331.)*

When a presumption of undue influence exists, it can actually muddy the waters. The burden of proof is not shifted but the accused must then offer evidence regarding the transaction(s) in question. It's a technical shift and one that is not well understood by most involved in these cases.

The corollary of these cases is the fact that they are very time consuming, involving significant discovery (i.e., fact finding) with subpoenas, depositions, evidentiary hearings, etc. And in the legal world, time is money.

Contesting the appointment of a guardian or conservator usually occurs when an adult child petitions the court for the appointment of a guardian or conservator over their senior parent. The parent can challenge the fact that they need a guardian or conservator and other children can contest whether the parent needs a guardian or conservator. There can also be contests regarding *who* should be the guardian and conservator. This is particularly common between siblings.

Again, capacity and capability is the issue here. In order to have the court appoint a guardian in Michigan,

The court may appoint a guardian if the court finds by clear and convincing evidence both that the individual for whom a guardian is sought is an incapacitated individual and the appointment is necessary as a means of providing continuing care and supervision of the incapacitated individual, with each finding supported separately on the record. Alternately, the court may dismiss the proceeding or enter another appropriate order. (MCL 700.5306)

These contests can be particularly brutal on the family because the parent is still alive. And if the parent is contesting the necessity of the appointment it's particularly hurtful, painful, and embarrassing to bring these cases. The "best" scenario is where the parent is unequivocally incompetent and unaware of the proceedings and the contest is over who will serve.

Challenging the acts or failure to act of a fiduciary is somewhat easier. A fiduciary is generally defined as

A person who manages money or property for another and who must exercise a standard of care in their management as prescribed by law or by operating document (ex: a will or trust document). Common probate fiduciaries include the executor or personal representative of an estate. A receiver in bankruptcy; a trustee of a trust, or conservator for a legally incapacitated adult. A trustee, for example, possesses a fiduciary responsibility to the beneficiaries of the trust to follow the terms of the trust and the requirements of applicable state law.

In probate litigation, the term fiduciary could refer to a personal representative of an estate, a trustee, a guardian, a conservator, or an agent under a durable power of attorney, or a patient advocate.

In these cases, an interested party is typically cl spending by the fiduciary, or the lack of distributioi lack of sufficient financial reporting. In guardiansl challenges would be regarding the care and custody ~~~~ ~~~~ much less common without a corresponding challenge to the financial fiduciary. Sadly, most petitioners are far less concerned about the care of their loved ones than they are about preserving their inheritance.

Challenges to reporting are somewhat easier in a conservatorship file because the fiduciary is required to submit financial reports to the court for approval. However, challenging the spending and reporting by a personal representative or trustee is more difficult.

Most probate estates in Michigan are unsupervised informal estates and the reporting requirements are minimal.

Within 91 days of appointment or other time specified by court rule, a personal representative, who is not a special personal representative or a successor to another representative who has previously discharged this duty, shall prepare an inventory of property owned by the decedent at the time of death, listing it with reasonable detail, and indicating as to each listed item, its fair market value as of the date of the decedent's death, and the type and amount of an encumbrance that may exist with reference to each listed item. (MCL 700.3706(1))

email request

rev

please tax to my email

sent

date/time

Resistance

then - ref law

This must be served on all presumptive distributees.

Prior to closing the estate, MCL 700.3954(1)(d) requires that the personal representative has "[f]urnished a full account in writing of the personal representative's administration to the distributees whose interest are affected by the administration. The account shall clearly state the amount paid out of the estate in fiduciary fees, attorney fees, and other professional fees." This is where most of the litigation comes from. Either the fiduciary fails to provide this report, or the distributees have issues with how the money was spent.

But the reporting requirements for a trustee shift dramatically under the MTC. For example, the primary reporting requirements are found in MCL 700.7814, which states, in particular:

> Sec. 7814(1) A trustee shall keep the qualified trust beneficiaries *reasonably informed* about the administration of the trust and of *the material facts* necessary for them to protect their interests. Unless unreasonable under the circumstances, a trustee shall promptly *respond to a trust beneficiary's request* for information related to the administration of the trust. (All underlining and italics added.)

Section 7814(2) continues: "A trustee shall do all of the following: (a) Upon the reasonable request of a trust beneficiary, promptly furnish to the trust beneficiary *a copy of the terms of the trust that describe or affect the trust beneficiary's interest* and relevant information about the trust property." (All underlining and italics added.)

And finally, Section 7814(3) states that

A trustee shall send to the distributees or perm *le?*
distributees of trust income or principal, and to
qualified or non qualified trust beneficiaries <u>wl</u>
<u>it,</u> at least annually and at the termination of th
a report of the trust property, liabilities, receipts, and
disbursement, including the source and amount of the
trustee's compensation, a listing of the trust property and,
if feasible, their respective market values, and, if applicable,
any disclosure required under section 7802(5). In the
trustee's discretion, the trustee may provide the report
to any trust beneficiary. Upon a vacancy in a trusteeship,
unless a co-trustee remains in office, a report shall be sent
to the qualified trust beneficiaries by the former trustee.
A personal representative, conservator, or guardian may
send the qualified trust beneficiaries a report on behalf of
a deceased or incapacitated trustee. (All underlining and
italics are added.)

As you can see, there are far fewer requirements for the
trustee to report. There are fewer people who are entitled to getting any reports, there are fewer requirements as to what information is reported, and there is no uniform reporting form. In fact,
notice that the trustee is only required to provide a qualified trust
beneficiary the portion of the trust document that applies to that
particular beneficiary's interest. Many people are quite <u>stunned</u>
to find out that the trust <u>reporting requirements are somewhat</u>
<u>vague and not submitted to the court for approval</u>, and if the
grantors are still alive, the beneficiaries are most likely not entitled to *any* reporting. All of these limited reporting requirements

to a substantial amount of distrust and eventually litigation. All of these potential legal challenges are discussed in more detail in Chapter 2.

II. Why Write This Book?

I have to admit that I have a love/hate relationship with probate litigation. The cases are very stressful on the parties and the attorneys. I completely understand the stress that clients are under, not just being involved in a lawsuit, but the fact that the parties are all family members adds a much deeper layer of emotional stress. Add to that the fact that many of the family dynamics and issues go back to childhood and may very well have been buried for the last 30 or 40 years until the litigation brought them back to life. But what's difficult to deal with as the lawyer is the fact that the clients quite often turn on the lawyer as well as the other parties. This seems counterintuitive and in fact this observation stumped me for a very long time. After all, I am most often their only advocate so why would they want to treat me badly? I believe that there are two primary reasons that clients become adversarial with the attorney. First, they are just plain in "battle mode" and everyone becomes a target. They are so overwhelmed by the emotions and stress of litigation that they can't detach and change their emotions towards "innocent" people. I think the other reason is that there are almost always two (or more) sides to a story and part of my job is giving them my honest opinion on the case and sometimes pointing the finger back at them. They don't always like the truth and the advice and it becomes a case of "shooting the messenger." While the lawyer's job is to advocate for the client in court regardless of their weak position, it's not their job to condone everything the client has done or wants to do if it's not in their best interest. By the end of almost every contested matter, I'm spent. I'm ready for it to be over and put it to rest. However ...

I do feel like I've been called to this area of practice. It certainly wasn't something I anticipated doing when I was in law school; in fact, I don't believe it was ever mentioned in law school. It wasn't until I stumbled across a few contested probate cases early in my career that I realized that they were interesting and that I seemed to have a natural affiliation for it. I realized that *I get it!* I really understand the basis of the conflict and I love to dig down deep to find the root of the disputes. Once I realized that it was my calling, I started working hard to become more knowledgeable and more skilled in that area. The majority of my contested matters come from other attorneys so I must be doing something right. So why write about it? Because every now and then a case comes along that makes me realize that it's my passion whether I want to admit it or not. I hope that this book gives you at least a better understanding about it, but ultimately I hope that you find it both interesting and informational. I also love to hear people's stories, which is why I co-created a podcast called "Life Studies" with my co-host Deb Hart, which you can find on Podbean.

As a practitioner, I've always been interested in figuring out what's driving each case. It not only helps me to understand what the client is feeling so that I can better serve them, but it also helps me in resolving their case to their satisfaction. By digging deeper, sometimes we can avoid or cut short litigation by finding a resolution that the courts either won't or can't grant but will make the client feel more satisfied or vindicated, for example dividing assets in a way that alters shares from what the will or trust expresses, or even getting an apology from a family member. If litigation becomes protracted, we can sometimes construct a settlement agreement that will stop the bleeding and get the parties back to their pre-litigation life, reducing significant stress for them.

While obtaining my post-graduate certificate in forensic psychology, I began to have many "aha moments" where the science and psychology that I was studying reminded me of certain cases I had worked on. Since forensic psychology is the study of the intersection of psychology and the law, it's primarily used in the criminal justice system, the family courts, and the juvenile system. But I found the connection to contested probate matters so overwhelmingly obvious that the concept for this book was born.

In addition to the many legal and procedural differences between probate litigation and other areas of litigation, by far the most unique and difficult part of practicing in probate litigation lies in the psychology of the cases. And that's why I'm writing this book. For anyone who has ever practiced in probate litigation or been involved in any probate litigation cases, they will find this book to be remarkably familiar and at the same time, remarkably enlightening. And for those who think they may want to become involved in this area of practice, this book will either convince them to practice in slip and fall cases, or be their beacon to something that will continuously challenge them and simultaneously reward them in their career.

So what tends to drive probate litigation cases? In my preparation for writing this book, I studied 34 specific cases in order to determine what the common factors are. I will address those factors in more detail in the appropriate chapters. However, in sum, I found the following characteristics in the cases I reviewed, breaking down the "causes" of each case by category, four of them being the primary categories:

Client Suicide: Of the 34 cases that I reviewed, two of the cases involved the client committing suicide. However, in both cases, the victims of suicide were white males over the age of 60, which is the number one demographic for suicide victims in the US.

Family History/Family Dynamics/Mental Illness/Addiction: This category refers to a history of mental illness, alcohol or substance abuse, emotional or physical abuse within the family. Out of the 34 cases I reviewed, 19 of the cases involved one or more of these issues (54%).

Special Issues/Blended Families/Co-Fiduciaries/Family Farm or Business/Absentee Beneficiaries or Lack of Beneficiaries: This category refers to situational issues such as blended families, the appointment of more than one fiduciary, family businesses or farms in the estate, absentee beneficiaries, or a lack of beneficiaries. Out of the 34 cases I reviewed, 25 of the cases involved one or more of these issues (74%).

Statutory or Case Law Issues/Procedural Issues/Settlement Issues: This category refers to issues involving statutory interpretation, challenges to a will or trust, settlement issues, and other legal-based problems. Out of the 34 cases I reviewed, 12 of the cases involved one or more of these issues (35%).

Even though I could readily identify certain commonalities in my probate litigation practice, categorizing their causes and looking at the statistics was very interesting. A whopping 74% of cases involved issues such as blended families, co-fiduciaries, family businesses, and either absentee or no beneficiaries! This will be covered in more detail in my chapter entitled "There's No Such Thing As "The Brady Bunch." But it means that many or most of the cases that fall into this category are completely preventable. With proper counsel and planning, disputes arising out of these situational hotbeds can be completely avoided.

Whether you are a lawyer who already practices in the area of estates, trusts, and probate litigation, a lawyer who is considering practicing in the area of estate, trusts, and probate litigation, or a person who is wondering if their estate or trust may end up in probate litigation, I hope you find this book interesting and instructive.

CHAPTER 2:

LEGAL AUTHORITY AND LITIGATION PROCEDURES

Introduction

"He got off on a technicality!" "They got him on a technicality." How many times have you heard this said about a criminal defendant being found not guilty of the crime that they have been charged with, or, conversely, being found guilty as charged? Typically one of these expressions is used when the person speaking thinks the verdict should have gone the other way. To lawyers, those "technicalities" are called *the law*. We study it. We practice it. We live and breathe by it. And we use the law to support our client's position as well as possible. Each area of practice has its own set of laws, and probate litigation is no different.

In this chapter we look at the laws applicable to probate litigation in Michigan and the process used to move a contested matter through the legal system and to its conclusion. At the end of the chapter we review a few cases that I've studied where using the law and the process made a large impact on the case. I realize that most readers want to read about the real life stories of ordinary people faced with drama and discord in their families. But for the lawyers who are reading this or those who are "hooked" by now, this chapter should pique their interest and give them a window of insight into why things sometimes turn out the way they do in courts. For me, this is probably my favorite chapter, because it's where I get to talk about what lawyers really get paid to do—know the law and rules, strategize for their client, and become the advisor and advocate for their position. My Golden Rule of probate litigation is to follow Kenny Rogers's advice in "The Gambler" regarding knowing when to hold your cards, fold your cards, or just run away! I hope this chapter is as interesting as it is educational.

Pertinent Authorities and How They Interact

The governing statutory authority over probate and estate matters is the Estates and Protected Individuals Code ("EPIC"), which was enacted in 2000. In addition to annual updates and clarifications, a major change to EPIC was the enactment of the Michigan Trust Code ("MTC"), which is found in Article VII of EPIC. EPIC is always the starting point when researching any legal question regarding probate, estates, and trusts. Because it is codified (passed by the legislature and signed into law), it's referred to sometimes as "black letter law." Depending on which side of the issue you have been hired to represent, you are either thrilled to find a section in EPIC that supports your position, or you are seriously disappointed to find out that it doesn't.

Once you find the applicable sections in EPIC, you will want to look at case law to either further support your interpretation and application of the black letter law, or look for case law that gives an interpretation in your favor. In order to understand case law, you must understand its source. In Michigan, each county has a probate court that would be considered the "trial court" level. This is the court that has original jurisdiction over probate, estate, and trust matters. This is the only court where you will have an opportunity to present your evidence and witnesses to support your position. The other trial courts would include district court and circuit courts. The trial courts do not create or publish case law. If you receive an unfavorable decision from the probate/trial court, you have 21 days from the date of the final order of the court to file an appeal. While there are some matters which would be appealed to the circuit court from the probate court, for simplicity we will assume that the case is appealable to the Court of Appeals. Once you are in the appellate process, the courts from this point forward rely on the transcript from the trial court hearing or trial, along with legal briefs from each party. You may request an oral argument if you wish to verbally add to your legal position in a few short words. The case will then be assigned to one of the three-judge panels of the Court of Appeals, which change a few times a year. Once the Court of Appeals has reviewed the case and possibly heard the oral arguments, they will write a written opinion. This is the first potential creation of case law. If the court titles their opinion as "published," then the opinion is binding on all lower courts. If the court titles their opinion as "unpublished," then the opinion is binding on the trial court that made the decision in that particular case, but suggestive to the other probate courts. In other words, trial courts must follow the decision in a published opinion but do not necessarily have to follow the decision in an unpublished opinion. To give you an idea of how many opinions are "published" each year by the Court of Appeals regarding probate, estates, and trusts, there are typically 40–50 opinions issued each year in this area of law, and typically between 0 and 2 opinions are published. And by the way, this is slightly more than the number of cases in which[1] the Court of Appeals reverses the trial court.

Whereas the majority of cases that are decided by the Court of Appeals are those where the aggrieved party was allowed to file the appeal "by right," meaning that they automatically had the right to appeal the decision under the court rules (in contrast to those cases that the aggrieved party only has the option of requesting "leave to appeal"), the Michigan Supreme Court is by permission only. In other words, the aggrieved party may file a request for an appeal, but the Supreme Court will decide whether or not they will take the case. As a result, it's very unusual to have an opinion come out of the Supreme Court on a probate, estate, or trust issue in any given year.

Getting back to the legal authority, the lawyer's job is to find case law that trumps the other party's case law and support's their own client's position. Paper covers rock, rock breaks scissors, scissors cut paper. Published case law overrides unpublished case law. Supreme Court case law overrides Court of Appeals case law, *but* the cases must actually be on point—the facts of the case cited

---

1 In probate, it's common to use the terms "hearing" and "trial" interchangeably when speaking about an evidentiary hearing or other dispositive hearing.

must be very close to your case and the legal issue must be very close to or the same as your case.

But getting legal authority for your position is only half the battle. You must also have working knowledge of the Michigan Court Rules of 1985 (the title of which is misleading because they are updated every year). You will never get to the judge if you don't understand the rules of filing the pleadings and process. The court rules are divided into chapters based on which court you are dealing with as well as subject matter. All lawyers must have a comfortable working knowledge of Chapters 1 and 2, General Provisions and Civil Procedure respectively. If you are working with an issue involving the probate court, you must also be familiar with Chapter 5 of the court rules. And the first rule of Chapter 5 is that all other court rules apply, except where there is an applicable rule in Chapter 5, then the Chapter 5 rule will apply. It's also important to check the back section of the court rules book to see if there are any additional local court rules that apply to your proceeding. To really master the craft of probate litigation, you can wow your friends with your understanding of MCR 5.125, which is four pages in 8-point-font defining "interested party" in probate matters. It is critical you include every person or entity who falls under this definition in all the notices, pleadings, and other various communications in the case. I follow the rule, "When in doubt, notice them out." The most interested parties I ever saw in one case numbered in the forties. Imagine having to mail that many copies of every single pleading in the case every single time. Ugh!

One of the "secrets" in the court system are the case codes. They aren't actually a secret; they just aren't known to the general population unless they've done some investigating. When I file a case, it's critical that I designate the correct case code for my request. That case code will then determine which documents need to be filed, which elements of the statute need to be met, and ultimately, what type of relief the court can grant. The Michigan probate case codes are as follows:

DA = decedents estates, supervised

DE = decedents estates, unsupervised

DH = determination of heirs

PE = small estates

TR = trust registration

TT = testamentary trusts

TV = inter-vivos trusts (grantor trusts)

CA = adult conservatorships

CY = minor conservatorships

DD = developmentally disabled guardianship

GA = adult guardianship

GL = limited guardianship for adults

GM = guardianship of minor

LG = limited guardianship of minor

PO = protective order

JA = judicial admission of DD adult

MI = mental illness and substance disorders brought under mental health code

CZ = a civil suit brought in probate court under MCR 5.101(c)

So, for example, if the case code on a file is 2021-12345-TV, we know that the case was filed in 2021, assigned the court case number 12345, and involves a testamentary trust, or a trust that was in effect during the grantor's or creator's lifetime.

You may have heard the probate courts referred to as courts of equity. What is a "court of equity?" Sometimes it is defined as: courts which administer justice according to the system of equity (or fairness), and don't necessarily result in a financial judgment or incarceration. They also have historically been called Courts of Chancery. With the merger of law and equity in the federal and most state courts, equity courts have been abolished, and the probate court can hear and decide cases that involve both monetary and non-monetary relief such as the appointment of a Guardian for a legally incapacitated adult. This definition is of little help, however; it helps to think of what type of relief you are seeking from the courts. In general terms, when seeking money damages, such as in a personal injury case, the courts of law would have been able to award such relief. But if you are seeking the court's action on a matter, for example the appointment of a guardian over someone or the settlement of a deceased estate, those actions are more equitable in nature and fall under the jurisdiction of the probate court.

Life Cycle of a Lawsuit in Probate Court

A. *Commencement*

The documents filed with the court to initiate a lawsuit and those filed during the lawsuit are called "Pleadings." We can generally define pleadings as the allegations or assertions by the parties to a lawsuit of their claims and defenses, with the purpose being to provide notice of what is to be expected at trial. Most people are familiar with the terms "Summons and Complaint," "Motions," etc. In probate you can either file an Application or a Petition, or you can file a civil action in which case you would use a Summons and Complaint. The technical differences between all these is irrelevant to the purposes of this book. To begin a lawsuit in probate court, the aggrieved party must file a petition, alleging the wrongdoing(s) of the other party, set forth who all the interested parties in the matter are, and the statutory authority upon which they are relying. Perhaps the most critical part of the petition is the relief requested, or remedy. You *must* make a request to the court for the action you want them to take.

This process requires much more skill than it appears. You must show your legal authority for the probate court to have jurisdiction over the case, and also why that particular county's probate court is the proper venue for the case. Next you must lay out the allegations which you are claiming violated some law or duties. You need to focus on legally relevant issues. Some petitions I've seen wander into the weeds and make allegations about completely irrelevant issues in some sort of attempt at a smear campaign. No, it's not legally relevant that the defendant cheated on their wife if you're alleging that he failed to serve annual accountings on the trust beneficiaries. And finally, you must understand what the court can and cannot do about it. While there is much talk in our society about frivolous lawsuits, filings in probate court must be *verified*, which means that they are signed with an oath that the signer has read the pleading and that the facts and allegations are true to the best of their knowledge. Serious penalties apply to both the client as well as the lawyer if the pleadings are later found to indeed be frivolous. Sanctions can include the dismissal of the case, the assessment of legal costs and fees, and for attorneys, a disciplinary action. I have actually seen the court order a lawyer to pay the other side's legal expenses of $20,000 because their claims were deemed to be frivolous!

So as an example, a petition in probate may include allegations of wrongdoing on the part of a trustee. The petition would list the actions taken or not taken by the trustee, and cite the portions of EPIC that indicate that the trustee has committed a breach of fiduciary duty. The request for relief would probably include the removal and replacement of the trustee, and possibly a repayment to the trust of funds that should not have been spent or distributed. It's important to note that the request for relief must also include the legal authority which supports the relief requested. Part of the attorney's job is to find out early in representation exactly what it is that the client is asking the court to order. If the relief sought is not authorized, then it would be considered frivolous, and most likely malpractice for the attorney to make such a request. As an example of requests that I've heard clients express, I've often heard the client say that they just want the court to make the other party admit that they lied or cheated. This is simply not a legally supported form of relief that the court can order, so don't bother asking for it.

Two other important points that should be made here: first, even if the case involves an act that may also be considered a crime (i.e., theft, conversion, embezzlement, etc.) the probate court is *not* a criminal court. In most cases, it is not even authorized to administer criminal remedies. I've said more times that I can count, "Nobody is going to jail here." When a particularly vigilant client is really looking for that pound of flesh, I advise them to talk to the police about it. If the police think that a crime has been committed, they will investigate and turn it over to the prosecutor's office to decide whether anyone will be charged criminally. Only once have I seen or heard of the police or prosecutor's office following up on the "tip." Second, most people have the delusional perception that they can get the court to order the other party to pay their legal fees. Aside from the fact that the majority of the time the other party wouldn't be collectible even if they did get an award for fees, it's important to understand that the general rule in the United States is that each party pays their own legal expenses. What do I mean by the other party being uncollectable? The reality is that most people do not have the funds on hand, or even enough other assets, to satisfy or pay off a judgment. So that's something to seriously consider before you spend money on a lawsuit that you may very well "win" in court but then not ever collect any money on the judgment. The only way a court can order one party to pay the legal expenses of the other party is if there is a "fee-shifting statute." A fee-shifting statute is literally that. It's a codified black letter law that *shifts* the obligation of paying your own legal fees to the other party. These are few and far between. Most of the existing fee-shifting statues are not mandatory, so the court is not required to order the fees be shifted. You can tell if the statute is mandatory or discretionary by looking for the words "shall" vs "may." The use of the word "shall" indicates that it's a requirement, and the use of the word "may" means that it's up to the court's discretion. The majority of the judges that I've practiced in front of are not very likely to order fee-shifting in discretionary cases. This is a very important issue for the attorney and client to discuss prior to litigation. Litigation gets very expensive, very quickly. If I say it once I say it two dozen times to the client *not* to have any expectation that their fees will be paid by anyone other than themselves. And yet, by the end of the case, many of them act like I told them just the opposite. The moral of this story is that you shouldn't file a lawsuit in probate court unless you're willing to bear the costs.

One final decision that should be made at the commencement of the case is whether you would like a bench trial or jury trial. Most civil cases use a jury trial system but it's very rare for a probate court to seat a jury. In fact, I testified as an expert witness in a probate jury trial and the judge said that it was the first jury trial they had had in that courtroom since the courthouse was built in the 1970s! The default is to have a bench trial. This means that the decisions will all be made by the probate judge. However, if the attorney feels that it is in the best interest of the client to have the case heard in front of a jury, then the request for a jury trial must be made within 28 days of the defendant's reply being filed. And yes, you have to pay a fee for that.

B. *Preliminary Hearing*

Typically when a petition is filed in the probate court to commence a suit, the filing attorney can obtain a hearing date from the court and serve the Notice of Hearing to the defendant and all interested parties at the same time as the petition. The defendant is not required to file a response, and may just show up at the hearing and announce their position. This is typically what happens when parties are unrepresented by counsel. Which is waaaaaayy too often in my opinion. If the parties are all in agreement on the requests made in the petition, this is called an "uncontested" petition, and the court may make a decision at that time. This is typically what happens in standard guardianship and conservatorship cases or formal proceedings to open an estate. But in our world, the opposing party will advise the court that they are not in agreement with the petition and the matter will be set for an evidentiary hearing (also known as a trial in other courts). Here's where probate litigation is quite different from most civil cases. In most civil cases, the court will set a scheduling conference for the purpose of setting dates for discovery, motions, pre-trial, and trial. If discovery is not requested in probate court, it is still allowed, but there is no cut-off date. If discovery is anticipated, it's a good idea to ask the court to issue a scheduling order so that discovery doesn't go on and on until the eve of trial. This is probably a good spot to also mention the appearance of the client in court. Even though the courts have been conducting hearings via video conferencing (e.g., Zoom), lawyers and clients should always present themselves to the court as if they are in person. This means that they should be showered and groomed appropriately, and dressed in clean, well-fitting, conservative clothes. I could go on and on about the variety of clothes I've seen in courts, but I'll just say that chewing gum and wearing an off the shoulder top like you're at a café in South Beach is not the ideal impression you want the court to have of your client.

C. Discovery

The time between the preliminary hearing and the trial is my favorite part of the case. Most of the work at this stage involves discovery, or fact finding. Most people have heard of Interrogatories, Affidavits, Subpoenas, and Depositions. These are some of the tools that lawyers use in the discovery process. Although it seems at times that the lawyers get a little out of control here and try to kill as many trees as possible and bill as many hours as possible, it should be noted that this process is heavily regulated by the court rules, and is extremely time consuming.

This is where the rubber meets the road and each side finds out just how strong or weak their case is. I personally love taking depositions. I love to have a conversation with the other party and any witness they may be using in their case. I usually walk through the pleadings with them and test their strength in terms of evidence and as a witness. Many cases are settled shortly after depositions when the lawyers figure out what their case may look like in a trial.

In general civil cases, such as automobile accidents, most of the parties are unrelated. Oftentimes one party is an insurance company and therefore the plaintiff and witnesses and possibly a medical expert will be deposed. But in probate litigation, the parties are by definition related. Taking the deposition of a family member while the other party/family member is sitting there can be a delicate task. Emotions are very high. Credibility between the parties is almost at zero. Not only will the deponent be very emotional and typically hostile, but many times your own client will be emotional and hostile as well because they will tend to think that every answer given by the deponent is a lie. In addition, nobody knows where the skeletons are hidden like family members, so quite often there are embarrassing facts disclosed. If there is a history of any type of abuse in the family, this is usually where that gets disclosed. Its uncomfortable for everyone in the room, including the attorneys, so it takes a special skill to conduct these types of depositions.

On the other hand, fact witnesses, such as the bank manager, a person who attended a memorial service, and experts such as physicians and psychologists are third parties to the case and are usually detached from the emotions of the case. Which brings me to the two types of witnesses: fact witnesses and opinion witnesses. Fact witnesses are those who can testify to what they actually saw happen, or what they were told (with some exceptions under the hearsay rule). These are the ordinary people, almost always family members. Opinion witnesses, however, can only be experts who can testify as to what standard procedures are, what the law is, or in some cases, are medical experts who can testify as to a person's medical and/or mental condition

cal experts are a key part of establishing whet

a guardian or conservator, or whether a pers

tary capacity to execute a document. Any exper

approved by the court before they testify during

attorney who brings the witness forward must

allow them to testify as an expert *on a particula*

must question the witness under oath as to thei

on that particular issue. The other attorneys then

tunity to cross-examine the expert as well. If the o

ney(s) do not believe that the witness is an expert t

ask the court not to allow the testimony. At that poi

will probably do further questioning of their credentia

a decision as to whether they qualify as an expert. M

however, the opposing attorney(s) ask a few questions

that the witness is qualified as an expert. This is *not* th

accepting the actual testimony as true! Once the witnes

fied as an expert, the opposing attorneys will cross-exam

as expected.

The goal of the opposing attorney is to try to discre

expert's testimony in some way, shape, or form, usually

ing to get them to admit that there are flaws in their analysi

there's no doubt, expert witnesses are very powerful to the

The equally difficult witnesses to handle are the fact witn

who are family members. While the expert witnesses are seasoned

professionals and emotionally detached from the proceedings,

the fact witnesses are typically in their first court action and very

emotionally involved. They can be extremely difficult to examine and cross-examine because they tend to answer questions in a multitude of ways, not always consistently and they tend to wander off into the weeds by expounding on all the lousy things their opposing party has done to them over the years, most of which have absolutely zero to do with the case at hand.

And what about those depositions and interrogatories that the parties went through? What good are those? All discovery requests (interrogatories, requests for production of documents, requests for admissions, etc.) are documents signed under oath. Therefore, they can be used at the trial to discredit or perjure a witness if their live testimony is different or contradictory to what the disclosed in discovery. Likewise, transcripts from a deposition (which you have to order and pay for and are not cheap) can also be used for such purposes. However, there is one form of deposition, a deposition *de bene esse* that can be taken for the purposes of trial, without the witness being present to testify. This is usually done if the witness is not going to be available for trial by reason of travel, work, or health, or some other cause. The deposition must be noticed out as a *de bene esse* deposition at its inception and all the rules of evidence will be applied accordingly. In other words, you can't take a standard deposition and then decide later that you are going to use it as evidence or testimony during the trial without the witness there.

One other note on discovery, using social media as evidence has become more and more prevalent over the last 15 years. Therefore, it's important to ask for any potential copies of social media during the discovery process. It still amazes me that users of social media are either ignorant of or just don't care that potential and current employers are looking at their social media, and that their posts can be used in court as evidence. I have been able to use copies of a party's Facebook posts to prove that the party was travelling to multiple vacation destinations with a person of the opposite gender whom they identified in discovery as just someone that knew their father and they had met once or twice. I've also had it used against my client for similar purposes. People! Watch what you post on social media! It never goes away!

D. *Memory Bias*

One issue that pervades litigation from the inception to the conclusion is memory bias. What do we mean by memory bias? Memory bias refers to the fact that human memory is never perfect, so we tend to remember events and things that people say slightly or significantly differently than what really happened. This is important because it can affect the initial pleadings filed in the lawsuit, the testimony of all witnesses, and the ability of the parties to reach an agreement to settle the matters. None of us recognizes memory bias. How could we? We recall events and conversations as our brain tells us to. To us, we *are* telling the truth exactly as it happened. This is in stark contrast to lying. If someone is lying, they *know* what the truth is and they are *intentionally* telling another version of the story. Because of memory bias, we can get three different recitations of the same event from three different witnesses. How different?

Research shows that people, "can even remember whole events that did not actually happen" (*Eyewitness Testimony and Memory Bias* by Cara Laney and Elizabeth Loftus, Reed College, University of California, Irvine ("Laney and Loftus") at Introduction). This can be particularly dangerous in criminal cases. "Faulty eyewitness testimony has been implicated in at least 75% of DNA exonerations cases—more than any other cause" (Laney and Loftus, at page 3). "Misinformation can be introduced into the memory of a witness between the time of seeing an event and reporting it later. Something as straightforward as which sort of traffic sign was in place at an intersection can be confused if subjects are exposed to erroneous information after the initial incident" (Laney and Loftus, at page 5). For example, if the witness is asked, "How fast was the car travelling when it passed the yield sign?" when in reality it was a stop sign and not a yield sign, the witness can easily believe that it was a yield sign in later testimony. "Subjects who had been asked about the yield sign were likely to pick the slide showing the yield sign, even though they had originally seen the slide with the stop sign. In other words, the misinformation in the leading question led to inaccurate memory" (Laney & Loftus at page 5). And unfortunately, "children and older adults can be even more susceptible" (Laney and Loftus at page 6).

What's critical for us in litigation is to understand that, "[e]ven slight differences in the wording of a question can lead to misinformation effects. Subjects in one study were more likely to say yes when asked, 'Did you see the broken headlight?' than when asked 'Did you see a broken headlight?'" (Laney and Loftus at page 6). And what's pertinent to probate litigation in particular is the fact that, "misinformation can corrupt memory even more easily when it is encountered in social situations" (Laney and Loftus at page 6). Because most conversations and experiences in family settings are more in the category of social situations than in a legal situation such as witnessing a car accident or crime, this can make memory more susceptible to corruption, which in turn will make witness testimony less reliable. To add to the likelihood of erroneous memory and testimony

> Subjects' accuracy was highly dependent on whether they had discussed the details previously. Their accuracy for items they had not previously discussed with their co-witnesses was 79%. But for items they had discussed, their accuracy dropped markedly to 34%. That is, subjects allowed their co-witnesses to corrupt their memories for what they had seen.

This study just confirms the simple game we all played called "telephone," where one person started a story and passed it to the next person and continued until the story was passed back to the originator. When the story was told to the originator, it was largely distorted! And since probate litigation primarily deals with family conflict, you can bet that many family members have had many conversations about each other's acts well before litigation ever begins.

In addition, "our expectations and beliefs about how the world works can have huge influences on our memories ... our memory systems take advantage of the recurring patterns by forming and using schemata, or memory templates" (Laney and Loftus at page 12). I've often seen this with clients as well. Clients or opposing parties will refuse to believe that a parent created an estate plan that is inconsistent with what the client or opposing party expected them to create. In those cases, they almost always claim that the plan was the product of undue influence and/or a lack of capacity. Likewise, if siblings are challenging another sibling's performance as a fiduciary, they are usually taking that position because the fiduciary has lied to them or fooled them about something in the past. That's not to say that the suspicions are never legitimate, but I've seen parties refuse to believe what is clearly disclosed in financial statements because of events that happened 30 or 40 years ago. When faced with factual evidence of that nature, they quickly make the assumption that there must be something hidden from them.

Lastly, the idea that people could develop "false memories" came about over the last 30 years or so when therapists were uncovering long-forgotten memories of patients' trauma. The patients would recall during therapy traumatic events, often times sexual assault, that they had never had a cognizant memory of before. The question then became whether this was truly a recovered memory or a "false" memory, produced as a result of the therapist's suggestions. In one study, researchers told students that they had talked to the students' family members and learned about four different events from the students' childhood—none of which had actually happened. Using short hints, researchers asked the students if they remembered each event and they were also asked to write about each event in a book. Students were interviewed twice regarding the events. One of the events was actually made up by the researcher and was verified by the family as never happening. After being told one story, one quarter of the students believed that the event had happened to them! In one study subjects were asked to review fake ads for Disney Vacations in order to convince the subjects that they had met Bugs Bunny at Disneyland. Of course this would be impossible since Bugs Bunny is a Warner Brothers character and not a Disney character, but some subjects did believe that they had met Bugs at Disneyland. "Importantly, once these false memories are implanted—whether through complex methods or simple ones—it is extremely difficult to tell them apart from true memories" (Laney and Loftus, page 14).

E. *Mediation and Settlement*

At some point before the hearing or trial, typically after discovery is conducted if it is conducted, the attorneys begin discussing the possibility of facilitative mediation or settlement. Once the parties have received the documents they have requested and/or conducted depositions and gathered the majority of the information they need, each side will have a much better idea of the strengths and weaknesses of each side's case. The most common result is that each party realizes (or should realize) that their position isn't as strong as they thought and that the other party's position is stronger than they thought. Something that good attorneys and all judges know all too well, there really are two sides to every story. This realization should help each party understand the risk they are taking if they try the case. And if they haven't been sticker-shocked yet by discovery, they should have a serious conversation with counsel regarding the expected costs of going to trial.

These reality checks should prime the pump for the parties to be open to managing their risk, stopping the bleeding, and trying to settle the case. There are a couple ways to do that.

First is simply negotiating a settlement agreement through the attorneys. This is cost-effective and works a small percentage of the time. I think it's often difficult for the client to make the mental switch from seeing their attorney as their full-on advocate and cheerleader to listening to their attorney now trying to convince them that their case has weaknesses and they would benefit from settling the case. Many clients will see this as selling out. My advice to the client is that the attorney's self-interest would be to continue forward and try the case, as this will generate the most income for the lawyer, regardless of the outcome of the case. So if the attorney is advising you to consider settling the case, understand that it's really in your best interest to consider that because you are the one who will be out the money and you may or may not ever recover it.

A more involved but more successful method of settling a case is to attend facilitative mediation. This is not to be confused with arbitration. In arbitration, the arbitrator stands in as the judge and makes the final decision on the case. I've never really figured out why a party would prefer to have a non-judge making a decision on their case instead of having the actual judge make the decision, but many industries provide for mandatory arbitration in their standard contracts. Probate is not one of them. Mediation involves a trained, neutral third party who facilitates discussion and settlement between the parties. This may or may not be a lawyer. While knowing the law on the case and even having experience with the judge on the case may be helpful for the mediator, it's not completely necessary. Many mediators are not lawyers, and many lawyers mediate cases involving issues that they do not practice in. Quite often just giving the parties a chance to express their concerns without the restrictions of evidentiary rules can help parties resolve issues that are not legal in nature.

It is critical to note that mediation is a completely confidential process. The mediator can only disclose information obtained by one side to the other side if the party who disclosed the information gives the mediator permission to disclose it. In addition, settlement offers and other details of discussions are not allowed to be presented in court. Lastly, the mediator cannot be called to testify in court. It's the Las Vegas rule—what happens in mediation stays in mediation. This helps encourage the parties to have an open and honest discussion with the mediator and to protect any information that is disclosed during mediation from being used in court.

Another benefit of mediation is that the parties can craft solutions that the court may not be able to. The courts are limited to remedies as provided in the statute, so many of the non-legal issues that are driving the case can be addressed and resolved in an agreement reached through mediation. As I alluded to above, the rules of evidence do not apply in mediation. Therefore, you can discuss documents and statements made by parties and non-parties that may not be admissible in court. Even if the parties do not come to an agreement during the first mediation session, oftentimes they will schedule a follow-up session or continue the negotiations through the attorneys. Depending on the research you look at, somewhere between 90–95% of cases resolve before trial, so mediation, arbitration, and settlement discussions are a critical part of the life cycle of a lawsuit.

Each mediator has their own style and their own procedures for mediating cases, but the process generally involves the mediator making some opening statements regarding the mediation process, the housekeeping rules, and what to expect during the mediation process. Then the parties are typically separated into groups by their respective position. Until the pandemic forced the use of remote participation by Zoom or other teleconferencing methods, the parties were placed in separate rooms with their attorneys, and the mediator would spend time with each group learning about their position and the strengths and weaknesses of the case.

Using Zoom or other teleconferencing tools, the parties can be separated into "breakout" rooms and the mediator can join or leave each room as needed. The goal is for the mediator to negotiate an agreement between the parties that they can all live with. Notice that I did not say that they are happy with. In contested matters, it's really unusual for one side to fully prevail on the case and the other side to fully lose on the case. This goes back to the fact that there are always two sides to a story. The problem in litigation is that you never know which side will prevail in court and which side won't, but chances are, each party will get a little of what they wanted, leaving each side feeling less thrilled than they envisioned feeling when they began litigation. Mediation and settlement is an opportunity for the parties to craft their own agreement, oftentimes with provisions that the court is simply not allowed to order, and they can control their risk. Controlling risk is probably the most pertinent reason I try to convey to clients when discussing settlements. While it seems obvious that trying to come to your own agreement is less risky than going to trial, the challenge faced by the attorney and the mediator is that each party does not accurately perceive the risk of their case. In other words, each party tends to think their case is stronger than it is and that the other side's case is weaker than it is. This is where a good mediator can bring that reality check to the parties.

In general civil cases and even in family law matters, there is rarely a question as to who attends mediation. In civil cases it's the plaintiff and defendant (i.e., the person harmed versus the insurance adjuster, or the husband versus the wife). But in probate cases, it's often more difficult to ascertain who should participate in mediation. On the one hand, any agreement the parties reach will have to be approved, or at least not objected to, by all the interested parties. Therefore, all interested parties must be invited to participate. If they do, then the agreement reached will be approved by all interested parties at the time the agreement is reached. However, if less than all of the interested parties participate, for example, if only one or two of the six children in the family are actively pursuing the claim, then maybe only those one or two children need to participate. Then the problem becomes how to get the remaining interested parties' agreement to the agreement. This can be done by calling the other interested parties, having them conference in if available, or by setting a hearing and allowing them to voice their objections at that time. The downside of this method is obviously that it's too late to go back to the drawing board if there are objections raised. This is a situation that the mediator will deal with prior to commencing mediation in order to avoid these procedural problems down the road.

One other issue that attorneys and mediators universally struggle with is outside influences. I consider outside influences to be anyone and anything that may distract, influence, sway, or hijack an actual interested party's perception of the case and ability to reasonably negotiate and settle a case. In addition to Google and other online research tools, lawyers and legal secretary friends, perhaps the most difficult outside influence that the attorneys and mediators often deal with in probate litigation and mediation are a party's spouse. Very often, the party's spouse is more emotionally fired up and is more of the driving force in the case. The actual party, being a family member, will quite often be somewhat hesitant to be so visceral and out for blood as the spouse. In our family, we jokingly call all the siblings' spouses the "outlaws" (as opposed to the "in-laws"). It's a joke, but it's a good thing to keep in mind when involved in probate litigation cases. So how do you deal with the outlaws in these cases? The court rules mandate that only interested parties attend mediation unless all parties agree otherwise. Under the court rules, a spouse is not an interested party. And if the spouse is an influencer, then many times the actual party will not want to participate in mediation without their spouse present. Attorneys and mediators will not want these outside influencers to be present because they will be an inhibitor to settlement. On the other hand, sometimes the spouse is the calming factor and the voice of reason so having them present is a positive situation. This is a delicate situation that the attorneys and mediator must address candidly outside of the clients' presence *prior* to mediation. Experienced and skilled probate litigation mediators are aware of this and resolve this issue one way or another well before the mediation date.

If a settlement is reached between the parties, either by negotiation through the attorneys or through mediation, a written settlement agreement will be prepared and signed by all interested parties. The agreement can either be entered with the court by way of a stipulation and order, or through a hearing on the record. Different situations will lend themselves better to each method, which is best decided by the attorneys. However, as an example, if there are several interested parties, or the parties are not geographically close, or if not all parties participated in mediation, it's easier from a practical perspective to just hold a hearing and put the agreement on the record. I also recommend this method if there is any sense that a party may come back later and try to claim that they didn't understand the agreement or the agreement didn't comport with the terms of what they agreed to. In general, while a stipulated order may be a faster and easier method, the hearing is definitely the safer method.

F. *Evidentiary Hearing/Trial*

So let's say that discovery has been completed, the parties are unable to reach an agreement through the attorneys and/or mediation has not resulted in a settlement. The parties will proceed to trial. And this is where the lawyers make a lot of money. Most people end up disappointed with the results of a trial, even if the court finds in their favor. Why? For many reasons. First, they don't realize that there aren't any "Perry Mason moments" (or for those of you who were addicted in the '80s, an "LA Law moment"). The court rules require full disclosure of evidence between the parties during the discovery process, and even require that additional information be disclosed if discovered after the discovery period has closed (that's a lot of "discovering"). If discovery has been completed properly, there should be no surprises at trial. And if a party attempts to introduce evidence or testimony at trial that was sought during discovery, it won't be admissible. So each side pretty much knows what the other side is going to present. It's not a question of surprising the other party; it's a question of how the court will perceive the evidence and interpret the law. This is a major disappointment for clients who were reluctant to settle because they so wanted to see that "Aha" or "Gotcha" moment.

Second, clients are almost always advised of the expense involved in preparing for trial as well as trying a case. While it's impossible to predict exactly how much it will cost to prepare and try a case, I don't recall ever quoting a client less than $10,000 just for those two phases of litigation. I've seen trials run anywhere from $10,000 to $500,000, and last anywhere from an hour to two or three straight weeks. And trial preparation is typically just as time consuming as the trial itself will be. And this is *after* all the discovery and negotiations have been completed. Yet, in spite of being advised on several occasions the cost of going to trial, the clients are still looking for that emotional satisfaction of winning at trial. Many times clients will proceed full steam ahead and say that, "it's not about the money." And yet, when trial is over and they feel that post-holiday deflation, somehow it *is* about the money. And they aren't happy about spending all that money for the results that they get. They discover what they were unable to accept before, which is, even if they win, they probably won't feel that satisfaction that they expected.

In addition, preparing for and trying a case is stressful. Not just for the attorneys but the clients as well. The emotional toll, the unknown, the family drama, and the time and money that are spent on the case become all-consuming and the clients pay a hefty toll for it. Going to trial against your family members is particularly stressful. Members of your own family are testifying in open court under oath about very personal events. Many times clients get extremely frustrated because a family member's testimony is inaccurate, or "a lie" in the client's mind. They don't understand why they can't just get up on the stand and tell the court that the other person lied, and that they should be arrested for perjury. This is where the evidentiary reality of trial comes in. It's very difficult for the client to understand that unless you have some kind of documentary evidence to prove the family member lied during their testimony (and getting up there and telling a different version of the story is not conclusive evidence) the client's testimony isn't necessarily any more persuasive than the family member's testimony. And memory bias can play a very large factor in a witness's testimony.

Every now and then there is a moment of surprise in the trial. And it's usually not a good surprise. Many times the plan to ambush the other side is a total flop, either by evidence entered that defeats the aha moment, or by convincing conflicting testimony, or some other reason. But typically, when there's a surprise in the courtroom, it's usually more of an "oh sh&*&&^" moment rather than a "gotcha" moment. Don't try a case in the hopes of finding that gotcha moment.

Preparing for trial is very time consuming. And for attorneys, time is money. Each side must walk through their case and map out the opening statements, the order of evidence and testimony, dealing with the other side's presentation of the case, and closing arguments. Every single move has to be planned out. The attorney has to make sure that they are proving their case according to the legal authority. They need to hit every element that the law requires. For example, in a case involving lack of capacity, the attorney for the petitioner must be able to prove that the decedent (in the case of a will or trust challenge) lacked one or more of the elements required to sign a will or trust, most importantly, *that the decedent lacked the legal capacity to sign the document at the time the document was signed.* This can be a difficult fact to prove, especially if the document was prepared by an attorney. How easy will it be to find an attorney who prepared a document to testify that the client lacked testamentary capacity at the time the document was signed? In other words, are they really going to admit to malpractice under oath?

Once the trial map has been laid out, the attorney needs to determine what order the evidence will be presented in, and how the evidence will be presented. Witness testimony? Do you need an expert? If so, can you qualify them as an expert in court? (And if so, do you know how much an expert witness charges for their review of the case and testimony in court?) How will your fact witnesses come across in court? Will they hold up under cross-examination? (Rumor has it that lawyers can be kind of nasty to opposing parties in court.) And what about the documentary evidence? How can you get that admitted? Most documents are considered hearsay and are therefore not admissible unless you have the drafter's testimony or can find some other exception to the hearsay rule. And let's not forget that social media can be admissible in certain situations, so how will that be admitted?

Finally, after planning for the presentation of the client's case, the attorney must prepare for the weaknesses of their client's case. Most clients don't believe that their case has any weaknesses, but every good attorney knows that they wouldn't be in court if there weren't strengths and weaknesses on both sides of the case.

What's the upside of going to trial? Sometimes the client literally just needs their day in court, regardless of the outcome. Some clients feel that they would rather hear the judge make a decision against them than risk agreeing to a settlement that would be more detrimental. Sometimes the client gets a better result from the court than they could have gotten in settlement. But each client must seriously examine whether any potential outcome and the risks thereof will be worth the emotional and financial cost of getting there.

Once the trial has concluded, the judge may issue a ruling at that time. If that's the case, a pre-written order may be presented to the judge for entry at that time. Or one of the attorneys may prepare the order at a later time and have the opposing attorney sign the order and submit it to the court for entry. Or one of the attorneys may prepare an order and submit it to the court and allow the opposing attorney seven days to object to the content of the order. And if the trial was lengthy or involved several issues, the judge may also "take the matter under advisement" and issue an opinion and order in the future.

Of course, every good attorney will advise the client that getting the order can be easy compared to enforcing the order. Depending on what the relief granted is, getting the opposing party to comply with the order can be a whole different story. If the order involves collecting money from the opposing party, always keep in mind what my first term law school instructor, the former Michigan Supreme Court Justice John Fitzgerald, said in Week 1 of class: "A lawsuit against an uninsured defendant isn't worth the paper it's printed on."

Deeper Dive

A common occurrence in probate litigation is a challenge to the validity of the decedent's will or trust based on the belief that the testator lacked the mental capacity to execute the will. Oftentimes the party challenging the will or trust is under the misconception that if the testator has been diagnosed as having any kind of dementia, memory problems, or cognitive impairment then the will or trust is automatically not valid. However, the testator's capacity is determined at the time that the will or trust is signed. For those who have cognitive or memory problems, or have been diagnosed with dementia, their testamentary capacity can vacillate from good to bad and everywhere in between depending on the time of day, the medications they take and when, or even the temperature. Therefore, a testator could lack capacity on one day, or even at a certain time of day, but have capacity at the time the document was signed. With many people, capacity is a moving target, not a fixed condition.

Given that fact, how do you go about proving a lack of testamentary capacity in court? According to EPIC section 2501(2)

An individual has sufficient mental capacity to make a will if all of the following requirements are met:

(a) the individual has the ability to understand that he or she is providing for the disposition of his or her property after death.

(b) the individual has the ability to know the nature and extent of her property.

(c) the individual knows the natural objects of his or her bounty.

(d) the individual has the ability to understand in a reasonable manner the general nature and effect of his or her act in signing the will.

Fortunately, the drafters of the MTC had mercy on us and set the requirements for creating, revoking, and amending a trust: "The same as that required to make a will in MCL 700" (7601).

In layman's terms, does the testator understand what their assets are and their approximate value? Do they know who their family members or natural heirs are? Do they understand that by signing their will or trust they are providing for the disposition of their assets after their death?

So how do you go about proving whether or not they had sufficient capacity? Well, the law starts with a presumption that they did have capacity, so anyone challenging the validity of the document will have to prove the lack of testamentary capacity by a preponderance of evidence. Those defending the document only have to show due execution. In evidentiary terms, how do you do that? The first place to start is with the witnesses to the document. With any luck they are still alive and competent, and you can track them down. That's not always the case. If the document was prepared by a lawyer, you'll need to track him or her down as well. But here's where it gets difficult. I have yet to find witnesses and or an attorney who will testify that the testator (now decedent) lacked testamentary capacity at the time the document was signed. Why would they? For an attorney, it would be admitting malpractice!

In addition to witness testimony you will need to obtain some form of medical records to support your claim. This, too, can be problematic for several reasons. First, the records may be so old that they aren't available from the provider. Second, with HIPAA laws, you probably are not allowed to get them without a waiver and release from the personal representative of the estate or by court order. And since the personal representative is most likely the person defending the document, they probably aren't very likely to sign a waiver and consent. So that takes you to the courthouse, asking the judge to sign an order releasing the records. But don't think you're out of the woods yet! If the medical records are not in your favor, you probably don't have a viable case. If the records do appear to be favorable to you, you will ultimately need the deposition and testimony of the treating provider. Again, are they available? In some situations, you will also want to bring in an expert witness who was not a treating provider (this is absolutely necessary if the records are not in your favor) to interpret the records in your favor. In case you haven't priced out the cost of medical records (no, they do not produce them for free), testimony from a treating provider (no, they aren't free either) and a third party expert witness (and your lawyer's time to handle all these moving pieces), you are quickly hitting tens of thousands of dollars. Before. You. Ever. Get. To. Trial.

As was mentioned before, a personal representative, guardian, and conservator are each court-appointed fiduciaries. And many times more than one person is interested in serving in one or more of these fiduciary roles. So how does the court decide who to appoint? Well it comes down to two basic elements: first, who has priority to be appointed under EPIC, and, second, are they "suitable" to serve? So let's look at what EPIC has to say about it.

> MCL 700.3202 (1) For either formal or informal proceedings, subject to subsection (2), persons who are not disqualified have priority for appointment as a general personal representative in the following order:

> (a) The person with priority as determined by a probated will including a person nominated by a power conferred in a will.

(b) The decedent's surviving spouse if the spouse is a devisee of the decedent.

(c) Other devisees of the decedent.

(d) The decedent's surviving spouse.

(e) Other heirs of the decedent.

(f) After 42 days after the decedent's death, the nominee of a creditor if the court finds the nominee suitable.

(g) After 63 days after the decedent's death, or if the court determines exigent circumstances exist, the state or county public administrator if any of the following apply:

(i) No interested person applied or petitioned for appointment of a personal representative within 63 days or the number of days determined by the court under this subdivision after the decedent's death.

(ii) The decedent died apparently leaving no known heirs.

(iii) There is no spouse, heir, or beneficiary under a will who is a United States resident and is entitled to a distributive share in the decedent's estate.

(2) An objection to the appointment of a personal representative may be made only in a formal proceeding. If an objection is made, the priorities prescribed by subsection (1) apply except in either of the following circumstances:

(a) If the estate appears to be more than adequate to meet exemptions and costs of administration but inadequate to discharge anticipated unsecured claims, on petition of creditors, the court may appoint any qualified person.

(b) If a devisee or heir who appears to have a substantial interest in the estate objects to the appointment of a person whose priority is not determined by will, the court may appoint a person who is acceptable to the devisees and heirs whose interests in the estate appear to be worth in total more than ½ of the probable distributable value or, if no person is acceptable to these devisees and heirs, any suitable person.

(3) A person entitled to letters under subsection (1)(b) to (e) may nominate a qualified person to act as personal representative. A person may renounce his or her right to nominate or to an appointment by filing an appropriate writing with the court. If 2 or more persons share a priority, those of them who do not renounce shall concur in nominating another act for them or in applying for appointment.

Wow, that's a lot of words to answer a short question! But if you drill down into the nitty gritty, you can usually eliminate most of the persons listed because someone will fit into one of the first few categories. This is another reason that preparing a will can be a huge benefit to your heirs and beneficiaries. Even if the ultimate distribution of your assets is consistent with the statutory intestate scheme, it certainly saves a lot of time, effort, and argument if you nominate your choice(s) of personal representative in the will.

But note a few key words that keep popping up throughout this section of EPIC: "disqualified" or "suitable" or "qualified." Unfortunately EPIC does not define these terms for us so we need to dig deeper. Sometimes disqualify means to take away from or deny qualifications or to determine one to be ineligible or unfit, as, in speaking of the 'disqualification' of a judge by reason of his interest in the case, of a juror by reason of his holding a fixed preconceived opinion, or of a candidate for public office by reason of non-residence, lack of statutory age, previous commission of crime, etc.

"Suitable" is defined as "Fit and appropriate for the end in view." "Qualified" is defined as

Adapted; fitted; entitled; susceptible; capable; competent; fitting; possessing legal power or capacity; eligible; as a qualified voter. applied to one who has taken the steps to prepare himself for an appointment or office, as by taking oath, giving bond, etc. One who has a particular status through some endowment, acquisition, or achievement, or it may describe one who has obtained appropriate legal power or capacity by taking an oath, completing a form, or complying with some other routine requirement. One who has mental or physical ability to perform requirements of job, office, or the like.

Sometimes it's easy to determine whether someone is qualified for certain jobs, for example, if there is an age requirement, form to fill out, or perhaps a required level of education required. However, when a court has to make a decision whether someone is qualified or suitable for a position that has minimal written qualifications and there are multiple persons who meet those qualifications, the decision as to whether they are suitable or not is much more subjective. Surprisingly, it wasn't until the 2017 decision in *Redd v Carney* (321 Mich App 398 (2017)) that a published opinion clarified suitability, at least for the role of a guardian. The court in that case echoed my statements above in that EPIC does not define the term, nor is there controlling authority defining the term in this context. The court began by looking at what the guardian's responsibilities are. It said that, "the overarching purpose of a guardian under EPIC is to provide 'for the ward's care, custody, and control'" (*Redd* at 407). After some exploration of other definitions and analysis, the court concluded that, "a 'suitable' guardian is one who is qualified and able to provide for the ward's care, custody, and control." (*Redd* at 408) And that is a question of fact. Each fiduciary position, of course, will have a different definition of what is suitable and who is qualified to serve. Obviously the requirements for fiduciaries who provide for care and custody will differ from the requirements and skill sets necessary for those fiduciaries whose role is to manage money and finances. Oftentimes the same person is qualified and suitable for both roles, but not always, and it's up to the courts to make findings as to whether each person is suitable for each role separately. A dissertation on the various definitions of suitability is beyond the scope of this book, but it's important to understand what the court will be looking for, and for our purposes, where conflicts flare up and cause litigation.

Definitely one of the top two causes of contested matters in probate is the lack of clear direction and requirements for financial reporting of trust assets and transactions. In the world of entitlement that we live in, this should come as no surprise. The surprise is usually on the family members when they find out how little, if any, information they are entitled to! Below is the section of the MTC which spells out the reporting that is required of a trustee to the beneficiaries. Keep in mind that one of the most appealing reasons that clients often choose to use a trust over just a will is privacy. From that perspective, I think the code delivers well.

MCL 700.7814 Duty to Inform and Report

Sec. 7814 (1) a trustee shall keep the qualified trust beneficiaries reasonably informed about the administration of the trust and of the material facts necessary for them to protect their interests. Unless unreasonable under the circumstances, a trustee shall promptly respond to a trust beneficiary's request for information related to the administration of the trust.

(2) A trustee shall do all of the following:

(a) upon the reasonable request of a trust beneficiary, promptly furnish to the trust beneficiary a copy of the terms of the trust that describe or affect the trust beneficiary's interest and relevant information about the trust property.

(b) Subject to subsection 6, within 63 days after accepting a trusteeship, notify the qualified trust beneficiaries of the acceptance, of the court in which the trust is registered, if it is registered, and of the trustee's name, address, and telephone number.

(c) Subject to subsection 6, within 63 days after the date the trustee acquires knowledge of the creation of an irrevocable trust, or the date the trustee acquires knowledge that a formerly revocable trust has become irrevocable, whether by the death of the settlor or otherwise, notify the qualified trust beneficiaries of the trust's existence, of the identity of the settlor or settlors, of the court in which the trust is registered, if it is registered, and of the right to request the copy of the terms of the trust that describe or affect the trust beneficiaries interests.

(d) Notify the qualified trust beneficiaries in advance of any change in the method or rate of the trustees compensation.

(3) A trustee shall send to the distributees or permissible distributees of trust income or principle, and to other qualified or non qualified trust beneficiaries who request it, at least annually and at the termination of the trust, a report of the trust property, liabilities, receipts, and disbursements, including the source and amount of the trustee's compensation, a listing of the trust property and, it feasible, their respective market values, and, if applicable,

any disclosure required under section 7802(5). In the trustee's discretion, the trustee may provide the report to any trust beneficiary. Upon a vacancy in a trusteeship, unless a cotrustee remains in office, a report shall be sent to the qualified trust beneficiaries by the former trustee. A personal representative, conservator, or guardian may send the qualified trust beneficiaries a report on behalf of a deceased or incapacitated trustee.

(4) If the terms of a trust direct that accounts and information may be provided to less than all qualified trust beneficiaries, at the court's direction, the trustee shall provide statements of account and other information to persons excluded under the terms of the trust to the extent and in the manner the court directs.

(5) A trust beneficiary may waive the right to a trustee's report or other information otherwise required to be furnished under this section. A trust beneficiary, with respect to future reports and other information, may withdraw a waiver previously given.

(6) Subsection (2)(b) and (c) applies only to a trustee who accepts a trusteeship, an irrevocable trust created, or a revocable trust that becomes irrevocable on or after the effective date of the amendatory act that added this section.

So, a few key words and phrases that lawyers will pick up on and delve into right away:

1. *Shall* is mandatory whereas *may* is discretionary/up to the trustee.

2. *Qualified* trust beneficiaries. Who is a qualified beneficiary and who is just a garden variety beneficiary? This is a legal term that has been argued many times and I have yet to find one clear answer. Sometimes the answer has to do with whether someone has a *currently vested interest* (i.e., is a current beneficiary), or whether they have a *contingent or future interest* (i.e., they may or may not ever have a right to a distribution from the trust depending on what order people die in). Nonetheless, this is often an area of contention that drives litigation. An authoritative analysis is beyond the scope and purpose of this book.

3. *Upon request*: In other words, you won't get it if you don't ask for it. This goes back to "you don't know what you don't know." Again, this stirs up controversy more times than not.

4. *Reasonable request.* What is reasonable? What is unreasonable? Does this refer to the method used for the request (email, mail, verbal, smoke signals, etc.)? Or does it refer to the number of times the request is made? Or what tone of voice is used in the request? Again, the discretionary nature of the language in EPIC drives litigation.

5. *Reasonably informed about the administration of the trust and of the material facts necessary for them to protect their interests.* I don't even know where to start on this sentence. I think any layperson can spot at least three problematic parts of this statement that would spark litigation.

6. *A report of the trust property, liabilities, receipts, and disbursements, including the source and amount of the trustee's compensation, a listing of the trust property and, if feasible, their respective market values, and, if applicable, any disclosure required under section 7802(5).* Note the use of the word "report." This gets many a trustee in trouble not only with the beneficiaries but with the court as well. In a probate estate, you are required to use the court approved form for the Inventory and Account of Fiduciary. Everyone has to use the same forms and everyone understands how to read them. But in trust administration, a report can come in any number of formats. Many times I am given nothing more than a printout from the trustee's QuickBooks program showing a list of assets or income and expenses totaled by category. One time, I was hired by a large national bank trust department to represent them in a contested court matter. We had to submit an accounting to the court. Well, EPIC doesn't require a court form for trust administration and the bank was involved because it was a large, complicated trust with multiple investments. They produced a 32-page transaction history with beginning and ending balances and virtually every transaction that had occurred during the accounting period. When I filed it with the court, the probate register rejected it because it wasn't on the court form. This became a battle between me and the probate register, whom I really didn't want to prove wrong since he yielded a lot of power to make my work life miserable; on the other hand, I couldn't really go back and tell a large national bank to fill out a little court form consolidating their 32-page report, either. I ended up asking the register to please show me in the court rules or EPIC where a trustee was required to use the court form so that I could go

back to the trustee and make the request. Of course I knew that he wouldn't be able to find it, so then I was off the hook without offending him. Too much.

7. *A copy of the terms of the trust that describe or affect the trust beneficiary's interest and relevant information about the trust property.* One of my favorite factoids lies in this sentence. Notice that the beneficiary is not entitled to receive the entire trust document. They are only entitled to receive the portion of the document that relates to their particular interest. I can't tell you how many times this issue has come up not just with clients and beneficiaries, but other lawyers as well. I've had to pull this code section out a few times to explain to the attorney that their client is not entitled to anything more than I have given them. Many of them do not believe me. All are frustrated and angry at me.

As you can see, just looking through this section of EPIC you can see a lot of red flags. What's a trustee to do? In general, I advise the trustees to do two key things: first, treat the trust administration like a probate estate administration and use the court form. Besides, it's easier than creating some other semblance of a report. Second, disclose, disclose, disclose. Most contested matters come about because a lack of transparency almost always leads to a lack of trust and serious suspicion towards the trustee. What is he/she hiding? What's the downside of using these rules of thumb? Well, if you disclose the entire contents of the trust, you may stir up a fight when a beneficiary sees what other people are receiving from the trust. And, ethically, does this fly in the face of the deceased's intent of privacy? There is no one-size-fits-all answer. Some attorneys I know take a hard line position and advise the trustee to only disclose the minimum amount necessary, even if this leads to a court battle. Others take the position that it's easier and promotes good faith if the trustee sends a copy of the entire trust to all beneficiaries with the first communication. As usual, I tend to drive down the middle of the road and have a detailed discussion with the trustee about the trust distribution terms and the family dynamics. It doesn't always work out perfectly but since we don't have a crystal ball, we make the best decision we can with the information we have at the time. In terms of financial reporting, not only do I recommend using the court form, but I also require my trustees to attach as much supporting documentation with their Inventory and Accountings as possible. This will also save time and challenges down the road.

What about undue influence? One of the leading cases in proving undue influence is *Kar v Hogan*, <u>399 Mich 529</u>, 554, 251 NW2d 77 (1976):

> Undue influence consists in persuasion carried to the point of overpowering the will, or such a control over the person in question as prevents him from acting intelligently, understandingly, and voluntarily, and in effect destroys his free agency and *constrains* him to do that which he would not have done if such control had not been exercised.

Similar to proving a lack of testamentary capacity, undue influence can be very difficult to prove as well. Again, it's difficult to prove what the decedent's frame of mind was at the time they signed the will or trust, and it's complicated by the fact that many times victims of undue influence have been isolated from family and friends for a period of time leading up to the document signing. And since undue influence has to exist at the time the document was signed, you are again looking to prove something that very few people witnessed, and it's usually the influencer who ends up being one of the witnesses, with the others hand-picked by the influencer. The chances of getting any of them to testify that the decedent was pressured into signing a document against their will is slim to none.

Thankfully, there is some help in proving undue influence as is described in *In re Erickson Estate*, 202 Mich App 329, 331. In certain situations, there is a *presumption* of undue influence, but don't get too excited. Once the three-prong test has been met to establish a presumption, the burden of proof doesn't actually shift to the accused influencer. The presumption merely requires the accused to offer evidence regarding the transaction(s) in question. Once they do that, the burden is still on the petitioner to ultimately prove that undue influence did, in fact, occur.

If you can establish a pretty firm case for undue influence, it is a nice option to have because it's so rare to have a true lack of capacity case. In reality, most foul play cases involving the execution of a testamentary document involve undue influence or its new cousin, exploitation of a vulnerable adult.

In Michigan, exploitation of a vulnerable adult is a more recent theory. It's also a very big deal. To the extent that the Michigan Attorney General has established an entire program dedicated to investigating and prosecuting such actions! The Attorney General's office is focused on the criminal acts of exploitation of a vulnerable adult while the probate disputes are civil actions. It's such a new concept, in fact, I alleged it in one of my cases and the opposing party told the court that such an action did not exist. Fortunately the judge was more up to speed than the attorney and he stated that exploitation of a vulnerable adult is, in fact, a cause of action. And truly, it's probably the most common bad act that we see with the elderly population. When you think about it, the action is essentially taking advantage of a vulnerable person.

"Vulnerable Adult" is defined in MCL 750.145m(u)(i) as "An individual age 18 or over who, because of age, developmental disability, mental illness, or physical disability requires supervision or personal care of lacks the personal and social skills required to live independently." And we commonly think of exploitation as: taking advantage of another for one's own gain or benefit. In probate cases, it's usually pretty easy to determine whether someone has received an advantage or benefit by their acts because it almost always involves money or another asset. The trickier part is identifying whether the adult was actually vulnerable, or knew what was going on and intended to make a gift even though it was unpopular with other family members. Unfortunately the transaction(s) in question are usually not discovered until after the vulnerable adult has passed away so determining the extent of their vulnerability and their intentions is difficult.

Common examples of exploitation of a vulnerable adult that I have seen and continue to see too often are someone adding their name to a bank account under the guise of being for convenience but keeping the money as a joint owner after the adult dies; gaining access to the vulnerable adult's accounts and using them to pay their own personal expenses; "helping" the vulnerable adult make changes to their will or trust usually to reduce a beneficiary's share while simultaneously increasing the "helper's" share; transferring any kind of asset (real estate, automobiles, bank accounts, etc.) into their own name (this may also be a basis for a conversion claim); "borrowing" an asset and later claiming that it was a gift from the vulnerable adult.

If you look at these types of claims—conversion, exploitation of a vulnerable adult, undue influence, and lack of capacity—you can see that there is somewhat of a continuum in the awareness of the person being taken advantage of. This is consistent with the natural progression of most people's aging. That's why these cases can be so difficult to prove. It's unusual, except in the case of a sudden traumatic event such as a stroke or brain injury, for someone to suffer a very rapid, very significant decline in their cognition and thought processing. So as a person progressively declines, they will have moments of cognitive malfunction, and then days of cognitive malfunction, then weeks, etc. And the legal theories reflect this. Conversion can be defined as the unauthorized exercise of the right of ownership over goods or personal property belonging to another, or the alteration of their condition or the exclusion of the owner's rights. This doesn't even require any decline in the cognitive ability of the rightful owner. For example, if I borrow a lawn mower or tools from my father but then just "forget" to bring them back for a period of time and he can't use them, this can be conversion. Moving down the cognition slope, undue influence and exploitation of a vulnerable adult are first cousins in a way. They both involve some level of impairment but don't have to rise to the level of a lack of testamentary capacity. With undue influence, the bad actor must have had so much influence or control over the victim that the victim made a decision or committed an act that was against their own wishes. With exploitation of a vulnerable adult, the victim didn't necessarily have to act against their own wishes, they just had to be taken advantage of. In many cases, there are multiple claims asserted in the same petition. For example, a bad actor may have committed multiple bad acts, or the acts may fit under the definition of more than one claim such as when a bad actor converts some personal items from the victim and also exploits the victim to gain assets. Commonly, the exact facts aren't known at the time the petition is filed so undue influence and exploitation of a vulnerable are both alleged and the petitioner may end up proving one or both or none of the claims.

Case Studies

Four cases that I researched will help illustrate the effect of procedure and the law in probate litigation.

One case I reviewed involved the statutory requirements of a fiduciary, in this case a personal representative of an estate. The fiduciary didn't understand that he was acting on behalf of the beneficiaries rather than himself. This is a common misconception. Many times the fiduciary understands that they are "in charge" but they confuse that concept with the fiduciary duty they have to the beneficiaries and the requirement that they don't self-deal. For example in this case, the fiduciary failed to prepare and serve reports on the beneficiaries (annual accountings) for many years, failed to administer and close the estate in an expeditious manner (went on for almost 15 years), and failed to treat estate assets as belonging to the beneficiaries rather than himself. In fact, the main asset of the estate was a piece of vacation property that he used exclusively for his and his family's own enjoyment. Worse yet, he transferred ownership of the property to a business entity of which he was the only owner, which is legally called "conversion."

In this case, the law was extremely helpful to the beneficiaries. Not only was the fiduciary removed, but he was also forced to provide the accountings for the previous eight years, and he was found guilty of conversion, which carries a statutory requirement of treble (triple) damages! But again, collection of the judgment is always a problem.

Another case I reviewed was the textbook example of mediation resulting in a resolution that the court simply would not have been able to reward. This case involved a person who was temporarily incapacitated so her durable power of attorney stepped in to make financial decisions for her. Once the person miraculously regained capacity, she was very upset with some of the acts of the fiduciary—namely, cleaning out her house and throwing some things away. She sued the fiduciary for significant damages that she probably could not substantiate in court, however, the fiduciary would be strapped with legal expenses of preparing for and going through a trial on the matter. Through mediation, the parties were able to resolve the case simply by requiring the fiduciary to write apologies for certain of her actions, which the fiduciary did while the parties were mediating. This saved thousands of dollars for each party, and resulted in a settlement that the court simply could not have awarded since there are no statutes that allow the court to use apologies as a remedy.

Another case involved a much more subtle act by a fiduciary, which most laypeople would not have known the consequences of. The successor trustee of the parent's trust had to make a decision regarding an annuity owned by the trust. He decided to reinvest the annuity into a new annuity, which then required him to designate a beneficiary. Rather than listing the trust as the beneficiary, he believed that he was doing his sisters a favor by listing them as the beneficiaries so that the annuities would pay out immediately and directly to them upon the mother's death. And that alone was not a bad idea. However, the problem came when he considered that payout as part of the sisters' share of the trust. In reality, by naming the sisters as the beneficiaries of the annuity, he had actually changed the testamentary plan of the parent because those assets would transfer by operation of law directly to the sisters rather than being added to the trust assets and divided equally between all three children. Not only is making a testamentary change for an incapacitated person outside the scope of the fiduciary's authority, but it also altered the calculation of the trust distributions. What was supposed to happen was that the sisters should have been allowed to keep the proceeds from the annuity as well as their one third share of the trust assets, thereby giving them a larger share than he got. Obviously the sisters were standing there with their hands out waiting for their larger share, which created lengthy litigation.

Finally, a case that made even the judge cringe at having to follow the law involved a contested guardian and conservator file. Adult Protective Services became involved when a woman with chronic health issues moved to an assisted living facility from a large home and decided to store most of her personal property in the modest-sized room at the facility. Her husband was right along with her and was no happier about protective services being involved than she was. Protective services filed petitions to have a third party guardian and conservator appointed for her, and her children were in agreement. However, there was no dispute that the woman did not lack mental capacity; she just struggled with chronic medical issues.

Fortunately for the woman, she sought legal counsel from a seasoned and savvy probate attorney who knew the law well. Two days before the hearing, the attorney prepared a power of attorney for health care and power of attorney for finances for the woman, and she designated her husband as her fiduciary. This gave the husband statutory priority to be appointed as guardian and conservator, and required the court to determine that the document was deficient in order to even appoint a guardian or conservator. After the lawyer's reciting the applicable statute to the court, the judge denied the petitions and stated that it was one of those times that his gut tells him one thing but the law tells him another, and he has to follow the law!

Conclusion

This chapter may have seemed to have gone off in the weeds for some readers, but it's really meat and potatoes of what lawyers do. Having deep knowledge, understanding, and experience in a particular area of law is such an advantage a lawyer has for themselves as well as for their clients. It might not seem glamorous and exciting for clients, and there aren't that many Perry Mason or aha moments, but using the law and the facts of each case to develop a strategy and work for a favorable outcome for the client is the most rewarding part of my job, and why I continue to practice in probate litigation despite the moments of mental and emotional anguish. And sometimes the victories I have aren't even very noticeable or even appreciated by the client, but I know what's a win and what's not, and the court and opposing attorneys do as well. So for the times that I don't get a thank you note or verbal appreciation (yes, that does happen the majority of the time; but when the client doesn't express appreciation it makes it feel like none of the clients appreciate the effort) must be content with my own knowledge of a victory no matter how small it is.

References

Eyewitness Testimony and Memory Bias by Cara Laney and Elizabeth Loftus; Reed College, University of California, Irvine (*Laney and Loftus*)

CHAPTER 3:

PSYCHOLOGY:

FAMILY HISTORY OF MENTAL ILLNESS,
ALCOHOL AND SUBSTANCE ABUSE, VERBAL,
PHYSICAL AND EMOTIONAL ABUSE, PTSD

I suppose it's a good idea to start with a background in mental illness, psychology, and the social history surrounding it. Mental illness can take on many forms and can exist in varying degrees of seriousness and disability. The primary types of mental illness that I have found to be impactful on families and what tend to drive probate litigation, include depression and anxiety disorders, alcohol and substance abuse, emotional, physical and sexual abuse—including bullying—schizophrenia and sexual assault. Each of these alone or in combination can contribute to or cause what we now categorize as post-traumatic stress disorder ("PTSD").

Historically, society has not dealt well with mental illnesses. For example, in Greece, "a mentally ill [family] member implies a hereditary, disabling condition in the bloodline and threatens [the family's] identity as an honorable unit." (The History of Mental

Illness From Skull Drills to 'Happy Pills'") Therefore treatment of the mentally ill in these cultures meant a life of hidden confinement or abandonment by one's family. Mentally ill vagrants were left alone to wander the streets so long as they did not cause any social disorder. Those who were deemed dangerous or unmanageable, both in family homes or on the streets, were given over to police and thrown in jails or dungeons, sometimes for life. Other cultures took a similar approach.

It wasn't until Dorthea Dix (1802–1887), a Boston schoolteacher, campaigned for humane care for mentally ill persons as a political concern that changes in public perception and policy changes began. Because of her efforts, each state was mandated to develop effective public mental hospitals, or state hospitals, all of which were intended to offer moral treatment. But this did not necessarily happen. And it wasn't until 1888 to 1939 that Sigmund Freud, an Austrian neurologist and psychiatrist, published 24 volumes regarding psychoanalytic theory. This was really some of the first attempts to understand and treat mental illness.

Social stigma regarding mental illness has really decreased over just the last 50 years. In my youth (1960s–1980s), there was an unspoken "don't ask, don't tell" policy that existed. The theory seemed to be that whatever happened in the privacy of your own house was nobody else's business. I recall noticing obvious signs of physical abuse on some children, yet the school did not intervene. Contrast that to our current policies of mandatory reporting and Child Protective Services ("CPS"). And the physical abuse was the only obvious and outward sign of abuse. Many children were suffering from physical, emotional, and/or sexual abuse as well. These children were not only terrified to tell anyone about the abuse, but their cries would have fallen on deaf ears.

One of the most eye-opening cases that I've seen get public attention is a Dansville, Michigan case of a wife who waited until her chronically drunk and abusive husband was passed out in bed, took her kids to the car, and torched the house, killing him while he slumbered. This story became quite famous not only through the publication of a true crime book called "The Burning Bed," but by the movie of the same name starring Farrah Fawcett Majors. The wife was one of the first in the country to use the defense we call "battered wife syndrome" where the spouse has been the victim of ongoing abuse and is literally brought to the breaking point. The defense is similar to self-defense and/or temporary insanity. It was groundbreaking in the fact that the result of the ongoing abuse was finally recognized as causing severe mental health issues.

But what was most alarming to me about this story was that the abuse was certainly no secret. The woman's in-laws not only knew about it but witnessed it. The woman's mother knew about it. And the woman cried for help not only with family members, but with the legal system. Yet nobody came through for her. The public philosophy was that what happens in the home stays in the home. The woman was told in several ways on several occasions that she had to live with her choice of marrying an abusive drunk and nobody was going to help her out. Sounds like something out of the 1940s or 1950s, doesn't it? Sadly it was the 1980s!

Fortunately we are now in a social and legal environment that encourages disclosure, requires reporting for certain professionals, and supports those struggling with mental illness through many community, government, and professional programs by the way of CPS, Community Mental Health ("CMH"), the "Me Too" movement, and various non-profit outreach programs. Even our local Ingham County Jail recognizes the connection between mental health issues and crime, and offers a trauma sensitive yoga class to its inmates.

For those who think that mental health issues are few and far between, "[i]n any given year, as many as 30% of the adults and 19% of the children and adolescents in the United States display serious psychological disturbances and are in need of clinical treatment." (Abnormal Psychology, by Comer, 9th edition) To better understand what those suffering from various mental illnesses are experiencing, I've given a short explanation of some of the most common disorders seen in the US.

Anxiety, Obsessive Compulsive Disorder, and Related Disorders

People who suffer from this group of disorders often feel a sense of fear—facing what appears to be a serious threat to their well-being, they react with the state of immediate alarm. In addition, they often feel anxiety—a vague sense of being in danger which causes increases in breathing, muscular tension, increased heart rate, etc. Anxiety disorders are the most common mental disorders in the United States. You may have heard of the term "victimization," which can occur when a person is the victim of any offense

78

ranging from burglary to rape, and it often produces a general sense of helplessness and increases the symptoms of depression. Women in our society are more likely than men to be victims, particularly of sexual assault and child abuse.

More extreme but similarly common mental disorders can be categorized as bipolar disorders. People who suffer from bipolar disorders feel extreme highs and lows. "They may talk rapidly and loudly, their conversations filled with jokes and efforts to be clever or, conversely, with complaints and verbal outbursts. To get an idea of how these people may behave, "[i]n the cognitive realm, people with mania usually show poor judgment and planning, as if they feel too good or move too fast to consider possible pitfalls. Filled with optimism, they rarely listen when others try to slow them down, interrupt their buying sprees, or prevent them from investing money unwisely. They may also hold an inflated opinion of themselves, and sometimes their self-esteem approaches grandiosity." (*Abnormal Psychology,* by Comer, 9th edition, Chapter 7)

Child Abuse

Child abuse has been defined as "the nonaccidental use of excessive physical or psychological force by an adult on a child, often with the intention of hurting or destroying the child." (*Abnormal Psychology* by Comer 9th edition, Chapter 17) Abusers are usually the child's parents, many of whom were abused themselves as children and have poor role models. "Studies suggest that the victims of child abuse may suffer both immediate and long-term psychological effects. Research has shown, for example, that they may have psychological symptoms such as anxiety, depression, or bed-wetting, and that they tend to display more performance and behavior problems in school." (*Abnormal Psychology* by Comer 9th edition, Chapter 17) Interestingly, child sexual abuse appears to be equally common across all socio-economic classes, races, and ethnic groups.

The long-term effects of childhood sexual abuse can include depression, guilt, shame, self-blame, eating disorders, somatic concerns, dissociative patterns, repression, denial, sexual problems, and relationship problems. Sexual assault survivors don't disclose the abuse for many reasons, including the avoidance of pain thinking about it, the fear of not being believed, or of being blamed, among other reasons.

I find it startling that 28–33% of women and 12–18% of men were victims of childhood or adolescent sexual abuse. Women who experienced familial abuse report higher current levels of depression and anxiety when thinking about the abuse. Depression is the most common long-term symptom. Survivors tend to display more self-destructive behaviors and experience more suicidal ideation and may have problems establishing interpersonal boundaries. This often results in victims believing that people they love will hurt them—they develop a severe lack of trust.

In 2016 the gymnastics world was turned on its head when the *Indianapolis Star* printed an expose on the USA Gymnastics program, alleging sexual abuse in its program and the leaders' failure to protect the athletes. It wasn't long before hundreds of former gymnasts came forward to support the allegations. In Michigan, several of them approached the Attorney General's office with their stories and the allegations took on a life of their own. Over the course of the next couple years, hundreds of gymnasts came forward alleging that the US Gymnastics program's medical doctor, Larry Nassar ("Nassar"), had been sexually abusing the gymnasts, couched as a legitimate medical procedure, for as long as 30 years. And it wasn't limited to USA Gymnastics. Since Nassar was a staff physician at Michigan State University in East Lansing, Michigan, in the sports medicine department, there were several victims that had been assaulted by Nassar as students as well. The web continued to spread out to the local gymnastics company called Twistars, where Nassar was the official physician for the gymnasts. Twistars was owned by a man named John Geddert ("Geddert"), who was also involved in the USA Gymnastics program. There was always speculation as to whether Geddert had any knowledge about Nassar's assaults, but it took until 2021 when they finally issued a warrant for him. On his way to turn himself in, he stopped at a rest area and committed suicide. I guess that was as much of a guilty plea as anything. One of the critical lessons that we have learned through the Larry Nassar tragedy is that children and teens very often do not disclose the abuse. This is a result of some of the traumatic effects of the abuse, which may include a sense of fear and vulnerability/powerlessness, betrayal, stigmatization or secrecy and shame, and traumatic sexualization by associating sex with fear, pain, and coercion.

The Nassar case was a textbook example of not only the victims hiding their secret out of both shame and the fear of not being believed, but also an example of how easily adults can be fooled by those who appear to be knowledgeable and in charge.

This abuse was happening with the athlete's parents in the exam room! He would position himself in a way that the parent could not see what he was doing. And he carried it off as a medical procedure! Many times the abuse was happening in his "home office" while the siblings and parents of the victims were downstairs with Nassar's wife and kids chatting away! Once the victims began coming forward, they all told stories of the guilt, shame, anxiety, and sexual and relationship complications that they are living with in adulthood. I highly recommend any of the articles and books written by the survivors as they are something hard to even wrap your head around.

Psychological Abuse (Including Bullying)

Psychological abuse includes severe rejection, excessive discipline, scapegoating, ridicule, isolation, and/or refusal to provide help for a child with psychological problems. Bullying can be included in this category as well, which is the "repeated infliction of force, threats, or coercion in order to intimidate, hurt, or dominate another less powerful person." (*Abnormal Psychology* by Comer, 9th edition Chapter 17) Types of bullying can include hitting, pushing, tripping, name calling, mean taunting, sexual comments, threatening, spreading rumors, posting embarrassing images (particularly on social media), and rejection from a group. Bullying is on the rise: 39% of people older than 50 were bullied as teenagers versus 47% of those younger than 50 who were bullied as teenagers.(*Abnormal Psychology* by Comer, 9th edition, Chapter 17) "The internet, texting and social media have become convenient tools for those who wish to stalk or bully others, express sexual exhibitionism or pursue pedophilic desires … A number of clinicians also worry that social networking can contribute to psychological dysfunctioning in certain cases."(*Abnormal Psychology* by Comer, 9th edition, Chapter 17)

Disorders of Trauma and Stress/ Post-Traumatic Stress Disorder ("PTSD")

Our body physically reacts to situations or demands that require us to change in some manner, or step outside our comfort zone. This is stress. With stress, there are two components: the stressor, or the event that creates the change, and the stress response, which is the individual's response to the change or demand. Stress symptoms may include heightened arousal, anxiety, mood problems, memory and orientation difficulties, and behavioral disturbances. "Ongoing victimization and abuse in the family—specifically child and spouse abuse—may also lead to psychological stress disorders. Because these forms of abuse may occur over the long term and violate family trust, many victims develop other symptoms and disorders as well … Almost any kind of stressor may trigger an adjustment disorder. Common ones are the breakup of a relationship, marital problems, business difficulties, and living in a crime-ridden neighborhood." (*Abnormal Psychology* by Comer, 9th edition, Chapter 6)

While we may affiliate PTSD with military veterans, which is no doubt a significant population of people suffering with the disorder, we can see that many other life situations cause it as well. The physical, emotional, and sexual abuse suffered by children and teens (as well as adults) contributes to a tremendous number of people's disorders. While it's outside the scope of this book to get into the physiological reactions to stress and PTSD, I highly recommend the book *The Body Keeps the Score* by Bessel van der Kolk.

Schizophrenia

While much less common but even more destructive is the disease schizophrenia. Again, the medical diagnoses and treatment and causes of this disease are far beyond the scope of this book, but the disease is marked by episodes of fatigue, personality changes, social withdrawal and isolation, paranoia, lack of emotion, insomnia, hallucinations, and sensitivity to light and noise, to name a few common symptoms. It can sometimes be linked to family stress, such as chronic expression of criticism, disapproval, and hostility toward each other and an intrusion on each other's privacy. However, its causes are much more complicated than just that. One thing is known, however, that it's highly disruptive to the patient suffering as well as to everyone in the family.

Schizophrenia tends to show symptoms in the patient's early 20s. Usually the patients are highly functioning and socially engaged prior to the onset of the disease. Locally there have been three cases in particular where the disease came on quickly and ended in tragic circumstances. In one case, the patient was a top student in high school and excelled in sports. He was on his way to a very bright future. As his symptoms began to emerge, his mother sought a diagnosis and treatment for him. She was able to get him treatment under a court order that needed to be renewed on a regular basis through the community health department. Treatment was quite successful. However, like many schizophrenia patients, he would not stay on the treatment program on his own. Unfortunately, his court order had not been renewed as it should have been and his treatments had been halted temporarily. Tragically, before the treatments were resumed, he experienced severe hallucinations and drove his car over a firefighter who was collecting money for a charitable cause that the department supports each year.

Another more recent case involved a local young man who was outgoing and hardworking and began experiencing symptoms as well. Unfortunately, before he could get properly treated, he also experienced hallucinations and killed an elderly neighbor, quite violently in fact.

And in the last month, a local young man began experiencing symptoms and killed his mother, father, and brother before getting adequate treatment.

I have been personally touched by the sadness of this disease, as one of my classmates and childhood neighbors developed symptoms shortly after we graduated from high school and began to wander, living from couch to couch, or on the street. He travelled from state to state for a period of time as well. His family tried in vain to help him, but he just wouldn't stay with treatment. Sadly, he was eventually found dead in a local abandoned building where he had been living and died from exposure in his mid-20s.

Alcohol and Substance Abuse

While alcohol and substance abuse are not described here as a mental illness, they do tend to dovetail into the other categories.

The alcohol and drug abuse are often the result of physical, emotional, and sexual abuses suffered by the now alcohol and substance abuser. A vicious cycle ensues resulting in more emotional, physical, and sexual abuse by the alcohol and substance abuser, often upon their own children and spouses. And we know that victims of those types of abuses tend to end up with mental illnesses such as anxiety, depression, PTSD, etc. Even absent a specific mental illness or corresponding physical, emotional, and sexual abuse, in my observation, where there has been alcohol or substance abuse there is also a severe disruption within the family, generally displaying itself as distrust, feelings of victimization, and family divisions.

So, with that mini lesson on a few common mental illnesses, what does it all have to do with probate litigation? In my case studies, 54% of the cases I reviewed contained a history of alcohol abuse, sexual abuse, hoarding, emotional and physical abuse, schizophrenia, and other quirky non-categorical family dynamics, with alcohol abuse being the single most categorical contributor and other family dynamics as the most common overall contributor. What do those cases look like?

In one case, upon the death of the surviving parent (which is typically when things start to go south), an estate was opened to administer and transfer the parent's assets. As was required, the executor prepared and submitted an inventory of estate assets and subsequently an accounting of the expenditures of the estate. Thus became a clear division of the family. On the one side were two children who had continued to live literally within 10 miles of where the parents raised them and were an everyday part of the parents' lives. They felt that they had carte blanche to administer the estate in literally whatever fashion they desired. They also used their own bank accounts to conduct estate business and then would make large withdrawals of even dollar amounts, such as $200 or $1,000, which are amounts that aren't typical of most purchases, from the estate or the decedent's accounts to "reimburse" themselves. One of the personal representatives lived in the decedent's house, so the utilities were paid from a personal bank account, but the amounts they reimbursed themselves for never really matched the invoices they provided. The other side consisted of an adult child who had moved out of state and was not involved in the everyday life of the parents, and one other child who was about 100 miles away, who sided with the out-of-state child. The distrust and spite between the two factions was measurable. There were all kinds of accusations thrown by each side. Accusations of sleeping with another child's spouse, of threating to kill another child, and of theft and conversion. And it didn't help that some of the children had spouses who thought it was their fight, and at times were even more venomous than the actual beneficiaries.

The legal fight revolved around objections to the fiduciary's accountings. There were volumes of documents discovered and reviewed in detail. There were depositions taken. There were evidentiary hearings on the matter. It took on a life of its own. And were they arguing over millions of dollars? Of course not! The estate was quite modest, yet you would think that they were fighting over Aretha Franklin's estate. The case was eventually settled between the parties, mostly because it was not cost-effective to continue litigating. But what went wrong?

Primarily what you had was an alcoholic parent. Many times people have an image of an alcoholic as the "town drunk" or the homeless person. But the majority of alcoholics are quite functional. In this situation, an outsider probably wouldn't have picked up on the fact that the parent was a lifelong alcohol abuser. He was a kind man, and ran his own business and owned his own home. But clearly there were patterns laid in the family that could not be ignored. The lack of trust between the siblings was the most obvious. That's also the most common element that I find in cases where there was an alcoholic parent. There was a division among the siblings, also a very common element of these cases. And there was an underlying competition between the siblings, possibly resentful of those who managed to move away from the home and the ongoing alcohol abuse? Possibly a lifelong competition for the parent's acknowledgement? Approval? Acceptance? Praise? Attention? And certainly a sense of entitlement on the part of those who had stayed close to, in their minds, take care of the parent.

Two other cases I studied also involved alcohol abuse. In one situation the parent was deceased and in the other the parent was still alive but incapacitated due to dementia. In that case, the legal battle took the form of a guardianship and conservatorship case. In the first case, the adult child had been living with the mother in her home under the auspices of "taking care of her." In reality, he was a lifelong alcoholic who couldn't keep a job, had lost his driver's license, and lived in filth in his mother's basement. Mom became an enabler. Once she was gone, however, the other siblings had no patience for the ne'er do well brother, and they had to take him to court to have him evicted. He left behind a disgusting mess in a house in disrepair, costing the already modest estate far more money than it could afford.

In the second case, the mother suffered from dementia and the father was already deceased. But that didn't keep the adult children from launching a marathon of lawsuits thinly veiled as guardianship and conservatorship cases. The bottom line was that none of the kids was particularly concerned with Mom's mental or physical health, but they were all tremendously concerned with who had legal authority over Mom's care, placement, and finances. Two of the three children were living in very nice homes owned by Mom, both in and out of state. Neither of them could have afforded the houses on their own. The distrust, hatred, spite, and vengeance these siblings had towards each other was over the top. Digging deeper it became evident that at least one if not both of the parents were lifelong alcoholics. And on top of that, they were financially successful and did not spare a dime when it came to their kids. So add enabling, pampering, and over-indulging to the effects of the alcoholism and you get one of the most dysfunctional families around.

The adult children apparently had no ethics, either. The case was such a mess that each side had worked with several different attorneys and law firms, leaving behind unpaid bills that exceeded six figures. Another complication in the case was that the trustee was an employee of the court so the case was moved to another county to avoid any potential conflict of interest. It was such a sad sight to see their mother in court, wearing her sunglasses and smiling, with absolutely no idea what was going on around her. It was shameful what her children were putting her through.

Hoarding

Hoarding may make for good TV, but it is actually a mental illness. Two of the cases I studied involved hoarders. A couple cases I've been involved in appeared to involve a hoarder or two, but the hoarding didn't appear to contribute to the family conflict, but rather it seemed to run in the family and become almost a lifestyle. One case I studied involved an older single woman who was very bright, very well educated, and very successful. She had formed a friendship with a woman at work for decades, going to social events together and even appointing the co-worker as her agent in her power of attorney documents for finances and medical decisions. Strangely, although many times over the years the friend had gone to events with the older woman, she never was invited inside her house. She would pull into the driveway and the older woman would be waiting in the driveway. And the garage door was never up. When the older woman had a serious health emergency and was hospitalized, the friend realized that she needed to make sure the house was in good enough condition for the older woman to be released from the hospital. What the friend discovered inside that house and garage was shocking! Not only was the house filled to the walls with boxes, furniture, mail, clothing, books, and literally anything else you could think of, it was filthy! There was old food and dirty dishes in the kitchen, along with mouse droppings throughout. The basement contained moldy items. And the garage was not only completely packed with items on every wall, there were even jars of "samples" from the older woman's professional medical and scientific work. After reeling from the sights (and smells) the friend was able to enlist professional and non-professional help to get the house in livable condition again. Most of us would be thrilled to come home to a clean and organized house—but not a hoarder! She was so upset and offended that she sued the friend for a breach of fiduciary duty and for compensation for all the items that were taken out of her home and disposed of.

The other case I studied involving a hoarder came about as two siblings serving as co-trustees of their parents' trust. This in and of itself can cause problems as you will read about in future chapters. However, the underlying distrust between the siblings and the complete inability to make rational decisions between them drove them to seek separate attorneys and litigate which one of them was suitable to serve alone as the trustee. It shouldn't go without mentioning that the third sibling was omitted from the trust and had no problems with that. That seemed like a red flag to me.

The parents owned two houses that backed up to each other. One had not been lived in for some unexplained reason but it did contain a modest amount of personal property including furniture, artwork and a Corvette. The main house was indescribable. Literally every inch of the floor was covered with boxes and furniture and other personal property except for a narrow walkway through the rooms and hallway so that they could move from room to room. Rooms that the adult children had lived in growing up were still exactly the way they had been the day the kids moved out over 30 years ago, and also contained boxes, furniture, clothing, pictures, etc. stacked from the floor to the ceiling. The hallways were lined with hanging clothes, many of which still had the tags on them. And the basement had some of the most incredible magazine collections from 50+ years earlier. One section of the basement was a storage area filled with jars of canned fruits and vegetables, the ages of which couldn't even be guesstimated. Maybe the strangest part of the situation was that the siblings gave no indication that they thought anything was strange. Maybe, as in other situations, the hoarding was passed on through the family and maybe their homes were just the same.

Conclusion

Not surprisingly, emotional, sexual, and physical abuse can forever change the dynamics of the family causing long-term effects that extend far beyond the life of the first generation. In the cases I studied involving these contributing factors, I found there were common patterns of distrust, division, and signs of victimization (defined as the psychological effects on victims, relationships between victims and offenders, the interactions between victims, etc.). The families appeared to be divided into different "sides" with some siblings on one "side" and other siblings on the other "side." It was very similar to partisan politics where each party is absolutely convinced that the other party is always lying, always scheming, and always doing everything they can to take advantage of the other side. And no amount of evidence is going to change their minds. This distrust leads to division among the family members, even if it means isolating one family member away from all the rest. Without the ability to have a rational conversation between the family members, the family turns to litigation to prove that they are right and to punish the other side. The fact that they are burning up their own inheritance by pursuing legal actions is irrelevant to them. Many claim that they "would rather pay their lawyer than pay their (brother, sister, fill in the blank)." And they continue to litigate, claiming that they don't care about the money. Until the case is over and they are left with a fraction of what they started with. Then they are angry that litigation was so expensive and they refuse to pay the lawyers.

As I indicated earlier, schizophrenia is a much rarer mental illness, but a very debilitating one. I only studied one case where schizophrenia seemed to be the underlying source of family dysfunction. Once again this case involved two parents who were still alive, wealthy, and in need of help. One parent was in advanced stage dementia and literally had no concept of where he was or who any of his kids were. The other parent was arguing that she was able to care for herself as well as for the husband. However, she suffered from a lifelong history of mental illness, including schizophrenia. The adult children were in a full force legal battle over control of the parents' placement and finances (sound familiar?). There was distrust, division, and isolation between the siblings. And there was enough money to go around. What I found most disturbing about this case was that one of the parents had not left the couch in 10 years. Hired help brought her food on a TV tray. She "bathed" herself out of a bottle of water. And she designed what she considered a smart way to toilet herself. She simply covered an area of the floor in front of her with newspaper, slid forward, relieved herself, rolled it up and had either her hired help or her demented husband take it out to the trash. You can't make this stuff up.

There were eight other cases that I studied that appeared to be driven by various forms of abuse, mental illness, and the like but they were too varied to really categorize into one source. But in each of those cases, it was obvious if you looked deep enough that the cracks were there long before the lawsuit was filed. The dynamics between the parties (i.e., usually siblings) were established by whatever dysfunction was present over the period of their childhood. Once the parent(s) was deceased, the crack became a full blown crevice and then a ravine.

References

Abnormal Psychology 9th Edition by Ronald J. Comer (*Abnormal Psychology 9th edition by Comer*)

The History of Mental Illness from Skull Drills to 'Happy Pills'; www.inquireisjournal.com/articles by A.M. Foerschner 2010 Volume 2, November 2009 (*The History of Mental Illness from Skull Drills to 'Happy Pills'*)

CHAPTER 4:

SITUATIONAL ROOTS AND CAUSES

(AKA THERE'S NO SUCH THING AS THE BRADY BUNCH)

What do blended families, co-fiduciaries, family businesses or farms, absentee beneficiaries, or a lack of beneficiaries have in common? Each of these situations seems completely innocuous, and each of them occur everywhere around us, and for many of us occurs in our own family. But these situations combined account for 74% of the cases that I studied. And they are easily preventable. I'll address each topic separately.

There's No Such Thing as the Brady Bunch

You're familiar with the iconic sitcom "The Brady Bunch" right? Single mom of three girls marries single man of three boys (no mention of what happened to the former spouses of Mike and Carol but we can assume that they conveniently died without causing any long-term trauma to the children). They have a fabulous live-in housekeeper, Alice (who wouldn't be giddy happy to have a live-in housekeeper and not have to work, right?). The kids have their occasional sibling squabbles, but overall, they all get along famously and there's no indication that they treated each other as step-siblings. And they all live happily ever after.

Mike and Carol would probably have been foolish enough to set up their estate plan as if they had never been married before and that all their children were each other's natural children: all to the surviving spouse for unlimited use during their remaining lifetime, then equally to the six children. What could go wrong?

Of the 25 cases that fall into the special issues category, 11 of them, almost one half of them, stem from blended families. Why is this? I think several reasons contribute to the fallouts. First, when a parent marries after a divorce from or death of the children's natural parent, the parent doesn't look to that new spouse as a "substitute" spouse. In other words, the parent looks to that subsequent marriage as being just as valid and just as meaningful (maybe even more so if the first marriage ended in divorce) as the marriage to the children's natural parent. In some cases I've seen, the subsequent marriage is stronger and longer lasting than the previous marriage and I've asked clients if they look at their subsequent marriage as their "real" marriage. This is a great situation for the parents, and typically the children from the first marriage are very happy for their parent to have found a loving and fulfilling relationship. However, make no mistake, the children from the previous marriage do not in any way feel that their step-parent is their "real" parent, regardless of how well they get along. Nor do they feel that their step-siblings are their "real" siblings. Therefore, treating them all like a nuclear family when a parent passes away is not going to sit well with them. Especially if there was any disparity between the assets brought into the subsequent marriage by each party.

Second, timing can be a big problem. Let's take a nuclear family. My parents are a great example. They have been together since they were 16 years old. They have been married for 70 years and had six children together. Literally their entire adult lives they have both contributed to their estate. If one were to pass away, there would be no other expectation than the survivor of them would be entitled to continue to live in whatever lifestyle they choose, even to the exhaustion of their combined estate. However, contrast that with a blended family. If one spouse passes away, it may be years before the surviving spouse passes away. And the surviving spouse may remarry. So based on a nuclear family estate plan, the surviving spouse would be able to use all the combined assets of their estate even to the exhaustion of the estate. Even if they re-married. And what if they surviving spouse remarries and then dies? Does the combined estate now become available to the subsequent surviving spouse? And whose children will eventually inherit what remains of the assets? Confused? Here's an example.

Amy and Bill marry and have four children. They divorce.

Amy marries Charlie. Charlie has two children. Amy and Charlie combine their assets to create one estate or trust even though Amy has contributed 70% of their combined estate from her own assets. They create an estate plan so that the survivor of them will have complete access to the remaining estate throughout their remaining lifetime, then any remaining assets will be divided equally between "their six children." The first issue you probably see is that Amy's children are not going to be happy that they have to "dilute" their share of Amy's assets with Charlie's two children since Amy contributed 70%.

Let's say that Amy dies and Charlie now remarries Desiree, who has three minor children. *Even if* Charlie does not mix and mingle the assets from Amy and Charlie's estate (which is now essentially all Charlie's estate), Desiree and her minor children will get the benefit of Amy's assets simply by way of Desiree being married to Charlie. And what happens when Charlie dies? Did he change his estate plan to now include Desiree's children? If so, you now have six angry children who don't think Desiree's three children should get any of Amy or Charlie's assets.

In an even more disastrous scenario, assume that Amy and Charlie didn't do any estate planning, or did not do an adequate job in planning for a blended family. As soon as either of them passes away, the children of the deceased spouse are no longer related to the surviving spouse, i.e., not heirs, etc., so dividing equally between the children doesn't mean all six children.

In Michigan, EPIC allows for a surviving spouse to make certain elections, the technical details of which are beyond the scope of this book, which can result in the surviving spouse taking all or the majority of the decedent's estate regardless of what a will or trust may provide for. And the heaviest hitters of all—designated beneficiaries—will override *everything* and potentially leave the decedent's heirs with nothing.

I realize that most people in a blended family who are reading this book are thinking, "It's a good thing my kids don't feel that way." I'm here to tell you that they may *not* feel that way, *now*. But when the second spouse passes away, the gloves come off. Let me give you a few real-life examples from the cases I studied.

In one case, the oldest child was the natural child of the wife but the step-child of the husband. Wife and husband had four natural children of their own. The parents and step-siblings always treated the oldest child as a natural child, and her biological father was never in the picture. When the children were all middle-aged adults, the wife/mother died. Ten days later, the husband/father met with his lawyer and changed the husband and wife's joint trust to exclude the oldest child. When the husband/father died, litigation ensued, to nobody's surprise.

The legal issue involved in the case was whether the father/husband had legal capacity and legal authority to make such an amendment to the joint trust. You see, only the grantor has the legal ability to amend a trust. Even though they were the same person, the legal distinction was critical and the court made the almost-never-made decision to void the amendment, thereby allowing all five of Mom's children to inherit rather than only Dad's four children.

This case showed a clear case of greed upon its inception. The fact that the other four children were unwilling to split the assets five ways instead of four, even though they admitted that they always felt that the oldest was a sibling just like the rest of them, was a clear indicator that they were going to hold their ground for their full share. And the trust assets were *not* substantial.

This case dragged on for much longer than necessary because they had a judge who didn't like litigation and refused to actually make a decision. Mediation failed as well. During the proceedings, which included several depositions in several different Michigan counties, it was disclosed that there had been sexual assault by one of the brothers against the oldest child. This had caused the oldest child to be unstable (yes, really) and somewhat distant from the family. The siblings were unaware of or chose to ignore this little family secret, and they resented the oldest child for moving away and "leaving" the family.

Eventually the court found an arguably lame way out of the case. The court decided that the amendment to exclude the oldest child was not valid because the husband had signed it as "Trustee" and not as "Grantor and Trustee." Technically a trustee cannot amend a trust so although it was the same person and the intent was clear, the Court threw out the amendment. By making that decision, the remaining siblings could file a malpractice case against the drafting attorney in order to recover the amounts they lost by sharing their distribution with the fifth sibling and their legal expenses. It was a long, expensive way to include a sibling who had been viciously excluded from her parents' trust by the person she always considered her father, especially since she distanced herself from the family because her half-brother sexually molested her.

Two other cases I examined were nice attempts to plan but the estate planning attorney must not have understood the dynamics of a blended family and clearly didn't anticipate the fall-out after the death of the first spouse. In one case of another blended family scenario gone wrong, the husband was married to his first wife for many years but they never had kids. He was very close to his wife's brothers, in fact, they treated him just like another brother. After his wife died he remarried a woman who had her own adult children. They lived in his house and used his northern Michigan cottage and acquired some assets together, including a new truck and some "toys" for the cottage. They also made several improvements on the cottage together.

The poor husband thought he was coming up with the perfect plan to provide for both his surviving spouse and his "brothers." He named one of the brothers as the personal representative of the estate, left his surviving spouse the house, and divided the tangible personal property and the cottage into thirds for each of the brothers and his surviving spouse. Seems simple enough?

The first complication came when one of the surviving brothers died and the personal representative of his estate had to step in on his behalf. Things got even more complicated because the deceased husband's personal representative wanted to do a bang-up job in listing literally every piece of personal property that the husband owned on the Inventory. This would require him to enter the home and do a detailed search. Things went south rather quickly. The gloves came off and the truth came out. The brothers never liked her and resented her replacing their sister. She didn't like them because they were greedy and mean to her.

She didn't want them coming in her house and many of the items listed on the Inventory were actually hers, or items that she and the husband had purchased together. To further muddy the waters, she exercised her statutory spousal allowances and exemptions that I referred to earlier to take a share over and above what the will left her. Then there was the issue of whether certain items that were purchased jointly but titled only in the husband's name were joint property or not. Namely, the $38K truck that she proved was paid for with joint funds (with joint contribution) but only titled in the husband's name.

Multiple trips to court didn't help. The judge was wishy-washy and changed her rulings, made unclear rulings, and just made things worse. In the end, the court issued an opinion and the lawyers had to decipher what it meant. The surviving spouse finally just threw in the towel. She was in her late 80s, exhausted, and spending too much money on the case. Her daughter and son-in-law were absolutely abusive by inserting themselves into the case and made things worse. It was really an unfortunate situation knowing that the husband had planned so carefully to show each of them how much they meant to him.

In another case that almost a mirrors the first scenario, the husband and wife were both previously married and had children from their respective first marriages. After their respective divorces, they married and lived a happy life for over 30 years until the husband passed away. They, too, believed that they had done all they needed to plan for each other upon the first spouse's demise and for all their children upon the death of the surviving spouse. There were just two glitches that caused significant issues for the surviving spouse wife. First was the fact that they prepared an estate plan as if they were a nuclear family. They pooled all their assets and provided unlimited access to the surviving spouse as he or she may see fit—even if it exhausted the estate. If there were any remaining assets in the estate upon the death of the surviving spouse, those assets would be divided equally between the children. And one of them had more children than the other. And one of them contributed a larger share of assets to the estate than the other. Again, we see the perceived inequity that each parent's children will see when some get shortchanged and the others receive a windfall.

The other glitch that created some issues was the fact that each of them had kept some separate assets in their own name and designated their own children as the beneficiaries. This was not in and of itself a bad idea. It was a good idea to get money out to the children of the first to die without having to wait for the surviving spouse to pass and the share would not be diluted by step-siblings. However, it did cause some rifts between the step-children and subsequently between the step-children and the surviving spouse. In spite of receiving separate assets from their natural father, some of the decedent's natural children were terrified that the surviving spouse would be a spendthrift and spend "all their inheritance." Reluctantly the surviving spouse agreed to provide accountings of the estate money, but it didn't negate the hard feelings; it actually increased them because then the step-children were able to monitor everything the surviving spouse spent. Again, proper planning with separate trusts and potentially a third-party trustee may have eased or eliminated the fall-out between the decedent's children and the surviving spouse.

The examples could go on and on but the main point is that blended families, even in the best situations, have underlying issues that need to be dealt with in the planning process and the parents need to be aware that their decisions may not have the desired result when they are gone.

Two are Better than One and Other Myths of Settling an Estate or Trust

It's understandable that parents don't want to over-burden their children with the work of settling a will, trust, or other estate. And there's no dispute that it's a lot of work. It's also understandable that parents don't want to show any favoritism or hurt any feelings when selecting a fiduciary. These are almost always the reasons that clients choose more than one personal representative or trustee to settle their estate. But, "because a will is in force only when somebody has died, it never takes effect while the one who made it is living" (Hebrews 9:17). In other words, no matter what good intentions the decedent may have had, they are not around to see the effects of their decision.

I cannot say that whenever there are multiple fiduciaries serving disputes will arise or that litigation will ensue. However, I can say that I see more problems with co-fiduciaries than not. For that reason, I will rarely if ever prepare documents naming co-fiduciaries. Disregarding disputes, disagreements, and litigation for a moment, the practicalities alone cause me to advise against it.

When you have two personal representatives serving together, all documents and filings must be signed by both fiduciaries. And financial institutions vary in their requirements for dual signatures, regardless of what the court has designated in the Letters of Authority. The same is true when you have co-trustees serving. If they aren't geographically close, or their work schedules don't sync, it can be a logistical nightmare to get anything done. Furthermore, if a dispute does arise, you have no tie-breaker.

But often there are co-fiduciary issues that lead to litigation. Two cases in particular that I studied show some of the unintended consequences of having multiple fiduciaries. In one case, the parents were successful business owners with four children, one of whom had a developmental disability. They owned multiple homes and they invested substantial amounts of money in publicly traded stocks and bonds, and held many of them in paper form. Many had also been converted to street accounts, but they were numerous no matter. Despite their best estate planning efforts, they created a mess. They each left a probate estate and they each left a trust estate. Then they named two of their four children as co-trustees. One lived out of state and was a professional; the other lived locally and worked in unskilled labor at best. The fourth had been written out of the estate and apparently wasn't bothered by that.

I never figured out what the root cause of the dysfunction was. Possibly alcohol abuse, possibly physical and emotional abuse, possibly the disability of the one child, possibly entitlement; it's never been made clear. But the children who were named as co-fiduciaries were a disaster together. The child who lived out of state and had a professional career seemed to be very controlling but wouldn't make a decision or give authority even for the smallest tasks to the other fiduciary. The local fiduciary seemed to either ignore the tasks at hand or bumbled through at best. Eventually the co-fiduciaries refused to speak to each other and had to get separate counsel. The local fiduciary even burned through two attorneys.

The out of state fiduciary was aggravated because they couldn't get the local fiduciary to do the paperwork for the money and stock transfers in a timely manner. The local fiduciary was frustrated because the parents owned two houses next to each other on the same street, both full of their personal effects, and the out of state fiduciary only made one visit to the house to take anything out. Four years later and the property remained in the homes and the homes could not be sold. The out of state fiduciary also refused to have anyone else remove the personal property or sell the home.

Each fiduciary filed competing petitions to have the other removed as fiduciary. One of the fiduciaries agreed to the appointment of a professional third-party fiduciary but the other one did not. The trial was adjourned so that they could try mediation. That didn't work. Further discussions resulted in what appeared to be an agreement, but one of the parties backed out after a verbal agreement was reached. The lawyers asked the court to put the matter back on the docket but the courts are so backed up there was no resolution in sight. The lawyers became the correspondence secretaries on this matter. After a period of time, the issues took on a life of their own. I'm sure neither fiduciary really remembers what started the breakdown in the working relation-ship but they both became so embroiled in it that settling the estate and trust came to a grinding halt. In the end, the court removed both trustees and appointed an independent professional trustee. This cost significantly more than if the siblings had cooperated with each other and extended the administration of the trust out even further in time. It really was a lose-lose situation.

As we saw discussed in Chapter 2—another case involving co-fiduciaries that went south and had other problems—the per-sonal representatives got around the logistical problem of coor-dinating their signatures on financial transactions by using their personal accounts and then "paying themselves back" with cash withdrawals from the fiduciary account. At a minimum this cre-ated an accounting disaster. The cash withdrawals did not line up with the expenses from the personal accounts; the receipts didn't quite substantiate the same numbers; and the fact that they would transfer funds from the estate account into their personal account was in essence a breach of fiduciary duty. Once in litigation the fiduciaries were forced to produce their personal financial records in order to try to support the payments that they claimed to be estate expenses.

In addition to the accounting and reporting problems, the co-fiduciaries created a large divide between the other two benefi-ciaries. Two alliances formed, with the fiduciaries on one side and the other beneficiaries on the other. There was literally no trust between either side. In fact, quite the opposite. Literally every-thing one side said or produced was immediately pronounced a lie or fraudulent by the other side. The train just kept picking up steam. By the time the legal matter was settled, the majority of the estate had been eaten up by legal expenses and all the parties were completely stressed out.

So, what's the advantage of only having one fiduciary? With one fiduciary there is only one signature required for any reporting or financial transactions. There is one decision maker for any conflicts. And there is one leader to guide the others through the process of settling the estate or trust. The fiduciary is free to enlist help, professional or otherwise, but the process is generally smoother, faster, more efficient, and less problematic than having multiple parties involved. You can avoid the situation of "too many cooks in the kitchen" as they say.

The Ties that Bind ... And Gag: Family Farms and Businesses

Family-owned businesses have been the backbone of American history and economics since our country was founded. When the early generations of a family came to this country and started a trade or business according to their skills and needs to survive, the business would thrive. When it was time to retire, the first generation would transfer the business over to the second generation, and so on. There are many wonderful things about a family business. The opportunity to work together as a family, the knowledge of having a career lined up for you, and working on something that has a purpose. But many family businesses don't have such a fairy tale story. In fact, some say that family businesses go from shirtsleeves to shirtsleeves in three generations, meaning that the first generation works hard, the second generation enjoys the fruits of the previous generation's labors, and the third generation ends up back in shirtsleeves trying to keep the business afloat after the second generation fails to work hard and lives in excess.

Even when a family business does thrive in multiple generations, the family dynamics can be strained at best. Each generation creates more bodies and families for the business to support. Each member of the family will differ in what they want to contribute to the business; each member will have different skill sets and work routines, but all will want to be paid the same. Choosing a different career route is sometimes difficult for a family member because of inside pressure or because staying in the family business is a more lucrative option. And the transition to the next generation might not go as planned. And many times the industry itself becomes stagnant or obsolete as has happened in the coal mining and foundry industries.

One staple of family businesses in American is farming. Farming presents many unique challenges, not the least of which is the fact that it requires a tremendous amount of work, a dedication to the business 24/7/365, and very unpredictable income. It is not for the faint of heart. I have studied several cases that involved the transition of a family farm to the next generation and two in particular stand out to me.

The first case involved a deceased widow who left three adult children, two daughters, one of whom lived in the Carolinas and co-owned a golf course, and one who lived locally and worked with her husband in a successful industrial business, and one son, who stayed on the family farm property.

It was no surprise that the son was given an opportunity to purchase the farm from the trust in order to cash out the daughters, and it's no surprise that he wouldn't comply. The son played the entitlement card and claimed that he was the one who stayed home to take care of the parents and to keep the farm going. The daughters had no problem with him staying on the farm, in fact they wanted him to keep it because they were only about 20 years from having it registered as a Centennial Farm. The problem was that the son didn't think he had to buy them out, and didn't think that he had to pay any reasonable value if he did have to buy them out.

Fortunately, the daughters understood that the son was actually a little developmentally slow and that the parents had always taken care of him and protected him. In fact, they recognized that the parents taught him how to survive on the farm so that he would always have a way to make a living and always have a home to live in. Of course, he was completely unaware of his cognitive deficiencies. He thought he was smarter than anyone and everyone else.

Eventually the siblings reached an agreement and were able to value the property and get him to cash them out. It was actually heartwarming that the daughters understood that his needs were different than theirs, and that his abilities were different than theirs and they did their best to make sure he was taken care of without completely sacrificing their own shares. But it took a while for the parties to get there. And it helped tremendously that each of the daughters was financially independent. This case could have had a very different outcome if all three of the kids needed and expected a full one-third share of the trust value because the vast majority of the trust value was locked into the farm. Alternatively, if either or both of the daughters had been or was interested in working the farm, it would have been much more difficult to determine not only the ownership interests for each party, but the decision-making structure. And eventually, there would need to be a succession plan in place for the transfer to the next generation.

The other case that held my attention involved a combination of corporate law, probate law, industry standards in the agricultural community, and in-laws. What could possibly go wrong here, lol? The main protagonist in this story was a widowed man in his late 80s. He had literally been born in the family farmhouse and farmed the land and intermittently ran a dairy operation throughout his entire life. His wife had passed away and he had one son. He constructed a small ranch house on a small parcel of property that was across the road from the main farmhouse, dairy barns, and tillable land so that his son and his family could live in the farmhouse.

Father and son grew crops to feed the dairy cows together, bought and repaired equipment together, and ran the dairy operation. They also built a large new barn together that straddled the property line of the parcel with the farmhouse and a parcel of tillable land. It didn't matter to them; they were family and they were in business together. They had no expectation of the property or farm operation changing ownership to anyone other than their own family members. All their income was split 50/50 and reported on their respective tax returns as such. They had no written contracts, no formal business entity, just their mutual agreement. Unfortunately, everything imploded in a matter of moments on the 4th of July when the son suffered a fatal heart attack. And of course he died without a will.

As it turned out, son's surviving wife didn't like living on the farm and had a job "in town" where she lived and kept their kids. Soon the status of their marriage as well as the ownership of the farm assets and property was all called into question. The wife claimed that she was entitled to everything—the farmland, the house, the equipment and every other asset that she could find—because the son didn't have a will and she was the surviving spouse.

However, the father was devastated by the loss of his son and furious about the claims made by the wife. During litigation, the father established that some of the property was still owned in his own name, including the parcel that was under part of the new barn that he and the son built. Clearly that would not go to the wife. However, the parcel with the farmhouse and remaining tillable land had been deeded over to the son with the understanding that the wife could make whatever improvements she wanted to the house. Instead, she packed up and moved to town. Long story short, the father was able to show that a partnership existed between the father and son in spite of the fact that there was no written partnership agreement or official entity formed. And when a general partner dies, the surviving partner receives the decedent's business property which would include the real estate that the house occupied and the barn that straddled the property lines and the milking equipment. Naturally the wife appealed but the Court of Appeal upheld the trial court's decision.

You've seen the bumper sticker, "We're out spending our children's inheritance!" It's usually stuck on the back of a luxury item such as a motor home, boat, or other large ticket item that a retired couple has purchased to enjoy the remainder of their life. It is, of course, meant as a joke. However, it's real for many families. The number of adult children, and even grandchildren, who feel a strong sense that they are entitled to their parents' or grandparents' assets when the older generation passes away is staggering. It's a very significant force that not only creates probate litigation, but often keeps fueling the fire in existing litigation. I really don't think most people recognize it for what it is because most people feel the entitlement to some extent without knowing it. Put another way, there is almost always an "expectation" that the children and grandchildren will inherit the older generations' estate and when that expectation is interrupted or interfered with, the underlying emotion of "entitlement" comes to the surface. Let me give you some examples.

I studied one case where the grandparent updated their 30-year-old estate plan shortly before their impending death because their spouse as well as one of their adult children had predeceased them. The grandparent chose to leave everything to her sole surviving adult child, much to the dismay of the deceased child's children (i.e., her grandchildren). This created not only litigation challenging the validity of the will, but also destroyed the relationship between the adult child and adult grandchildren. Why? Because there had been an *expectation* based on the previous will as well as commonly known laws of intestacy that the grandchildren would inherit the predeceased adult child's share. When this expectation was not met, there was immediate suspicion surrounding the validity of the last will. The legal challenge, as it usually does, took on a life of its own, and the parties became more entrenched in their positions. The more the surviving adult child dug in their feet and refused to move, the more the grandchildren became enraged and felt that they had been ripped off.

Now, as the reader who is not emotionally involved in this battle, step back and think about this. Isn't an inheritance a windfall? Does anyone ever really do anything to earn or deserve someone else's assets when they die? Not that I know of. Unfortunately when an expectation isn't met, no matter how reasonable it is, the expectation becomes disappointment and disappointment becomes anger. And when hope and expectations meet greed, they create the attitude of entitlement. Where, "I hope Grandma remembers me in her will" becomes, "I deserve to get my mother's share."

In another case I found, one of the trust beneficiaries passed away four years into the administration of the trust. He had received several distributions over those four years and when he passed away, that money passed to his surviving spouse. However, there were two more remaining distributions to be made. The first of those was distributed equally between his three surviving children. But much to everyone's surprise, one more estranged child (who many family members didn't even know about) came forward and filed a lawsuit claiming a one-fourth share in the remaining distributions. In this case, I'm not even sure there was an expectation; he just moved directly into entitlement mode. After all, how can you justify that you should receive a share of someone's assets when you literally had no relationship with this person?

Or maybe the estranged child felt entitled *because* he didn't have a relationship with his father. In this case, there was also a question as to whether *any* of the surviving children should receive the assets since his estate was left to his surviving spouse. At any rate, the parties were smart enough to figure out that they should all compromise and they reached an agreement to save diminution of the value of the trust assets.

When There's No One to Argue

The last topic in this chapter may come as a surprise to you because all previous topics and cases have involved disagreements between children/siblings when the parents have died. So logic would say that if a couple has no children, there is nobody to argue. But these next two cases will show you otherwise. In fact, when there are no children of the decedent, many of the family dynamics are removed and the litigation looks a little more like a general civil suit and the parties can be equally vicious.

One case that caught my attention involved a couple who never had children and their only living heirs were three siblings (two siblings of the wife and one sibling of the brother) all of whom were of retirement age. The husband passed away first without much fanfare. His 80+-year-old widow continued to live at home until her death; however, she had started to exhibit signs of memory loss and possibly dementia. Her husband had been a pharmacist and together they built a very successful pharmacy business. The husband was a graduate of a state university and the wife was a graduate of a local business school, Both institutions were beneficiaries of the trust.

Initially the husband's siblings were beneficiaries as well. But not long before her death, the wife changed the beneficiaries on her investment accounts and the trust. The siblings were removed and only the charities were named as beneficiaries. Entitlement reared its ugly head and the decedent's siblings screamed "foul" and litigation ensued.

This was a $10 million estate so there was plenty of reason to keep the lawsuit going. Of course the colleges had counsel since they had a big stake in the fight as well. What went wrong? Capacity was one issue. Even though the wife was still able to live alone, those closest to her reported that she was developing dementia. The medical reports were inconclusive. As is typical of so many elderly people, the cognitive decline can be very slow and very inconsistent. And even an outright diagnosis of dementia does not make a person lack testamentary capacity in and of itself. So capacity was a big issue and there was no clear answer. Another issue was the alleged undue influence on the part of her investment advisor. After the husband died, the long-time advisor watched over the wife and made sure she got where she needed to be and helped her with her house and major purchases, such as the Cadillac that she wanted. What made the advisor seem like a very suspicious character and what met one of the elements of undue influence in his behavior was the fact that the new trust required the trustee to keep all the investments with that particular advisor even after both spouses passed away. With managed money accounts, the advisor could pretty much have a guaranteed a six-figure income just off the couple's accounts.

After a very long and laborious battle (I can't even guestimate the amount of attorney fees incurred with all the different parties represented—some by multiple counsel), the parties reached an agreement. The colleges retained the majority of the trust assets, but those entitled little siblings got a cut as well. It's just my opinion, but filing a lawsuit to claim a share of your sibling's estate when the decedent sibling left everything to charities is a special kind of entitlement.

As you can see in this case, the lack of children actually made things worse. Had the couple had children or grandchildren, they most likely would not have named the charities and/or their siblings as the only beneficiaries. And if the changes to the beneficiaries and the trust amendment were found to be invalid due to either a lack of testamentary capacity or undue influence, the children and grandchildren would have been the natural heirs of the couple anyway.

The second case I was drawn to was truly a textbook case of the "trophy wife." In this case an elderly man hired a much younger woman to be his ailing and invalid wife's caretaker. The caretaker was a generation younger than the elderly couple and the couple had no children. After the elderly wife died, the husband married the caretaker, who went through an impressive transformation from frumpy-dumpy "meh" to marvelous! Highlighted and stylish hair, manicured nails, fashionable clothes, and a very high-end custom vehicle. Otherwise known as a trophy wife.

By the time the elderly husband died, the trophy wife had retitled his financial accounts to make them jointly owned with rights of survivorship, changed the designated beneficiary on his accounts to herself, and gotten him to amend his trust so that she would receive everything else. Since there were no children or grandchildren cut out in the process, she may have thought, "No harm no foul." But the elderly man's nieces and nephews thought otherwise. They filed suit against her claiming lack of capacity and undue influence. Unfortunately the court had denied the nieces' and nephews' request to freeze the accounts and assets until the litigation was completed thus allowing the trophy wife to make "gifts" to her friends and family, including purchasing a house for her boyfriend. She spent down and gifted almost all of the assets during the period of litigation. Sadly, the trophy wife lost her case in a jury trial and was sued for all the funds she gave away. The Court of Appeals was involved; bankruptcy was involved; and it had a very ugly ending for everyone. So again, having those natural heirs/children/grandchildren can sometimes help avoid litigation.

Conclusion

Again, of the cases that I studied, this group of special issues accounts for almost three quarters of the underlying catalysts for litigation. I find that because I litigate cases like these, I am a better estate planner and document drafter. I find that the vast majority of litigation cases could have been avoided, and therefore many future litigation cases will be avoided, by making the estate planning client aware of these potential pitfalls and allowing them to tailor their plan accordingly. I find that in talking through these topics during the planning stage, most clients have never even thought of these scenarios. They truly appreciate me bringing the issues up and helping them think through and plan for not just possible litigation, but hurt feelings as well. And that, I believe is a very important and rewarding part of my job.

CHAPTER 5:

SOCIAL MEDIA'S EFFECT ON LITIGATION AND PRACTICING LAW

Introduction

The first time I heard the term Facebook was when one of my young adult children mentioned that their dad was on Facebook. I did a little investigating and found out that Facebook was a website that was designed for college students to communicate and keep in touch with each other. It was a semi-public forum in that you had to send a "friend request" to someone and they had to "accept" your friend request in order for the two of you to be able to "write on their wall" or "share a post." The more I learned about it, the happier I was that it was for students and not adults.

However, it didn't take long (like 6–12 months) for me to decide that I wanted to enter the Facebook world. Not because I wanted to keep in touch with college students or spy on what my kids were doing in cyberworld, but because I kept hearing of more and more of my friends and family members extolling its virtues.

I finally took the plunge one weekend when I had been trying to find one of my college roommates. I spent about an hour sitting down with my son learning how to set up an account, create a profile, and make friend requests. I was fascinated by the fact that once my account was set up, Facebook would notify me of others who I "might know" based on the information I provided in my setup and profile. Now, of course, I understand the scary truth of just how much Facebook sees and hears about me and my life and always seems to have just the right people and products popping up on my page. In fact, that very first day I was using Facebook, an old friend that I hadn't seen in 30 years popped up as someone I might know, so I sent a friend request. I wasn't even sure he would remember me. He did, and he accepted my request. As it turned out, we were both divorced and working within a few miles of each other. Long story short, we met for dinner and were married 18 months later! And that's the happy side of Facebook.

Since then, 10 years ago now, I have learned so much more about the scope and power of not only Facebook, but social media in general. Social media is sometimes defined as websites and apps that allow users to create and share content or to participate in social networking,. I would list a few examples of the numerous social media sites available but the list would grow exponentially just in the amount of time it takes to get this book published. "Social" media has almost become a misnomer, however, in that it has become just as powerful and just as important in the working and professional world as it is in the personal and individual's social world. Not only have business and service providers been forced to develop and maintain a website in order to be taken seriously, but they also have to have profiles on multiple social media sites, such as LinkedIn and Facebook even if they are not a self-employed service provider. Further, each industry has its own specialized social media platforms, such as AVVO and LawFinder, that focus on professionals in particular industries. And Google is kind enough to create a page for your business, whether you choose to keep it current and accurate or not. Like it or not, social media is here to stay and you either have to embrace it or get out of the game. Just like time and money, you either mange it or it manages you. It can be the best marketing tool you ever used, or it can be the fiercest dragon that you ever had to slay. Not only will people use it to assess your credibility, your skills, and your experience, they will use it to announce their opinion of you and your skills once they have done business with you, and there are apparently no rules that say their posts have to be truthful. And every successful business owner and professional understands the power of word-of-mouth marketing.

Because social media has become such an overwhelming part of our personal and professional lives, it has impacted our relationships with family members, impacted our psyches, impacted how we get into and try lawsuits, and often how we settle them. In this chapter, we will look at how we use social media in litigation, how we use social media as evidence, the effects of social media on our psyche, and how it effects the way we do business and practice defensive law.

Social Media as it Relates to Litigation

In order to understand how social media and litigation interact, we have to look at the various ways that people use social media in their personal and professional lives. Unfortunately, there are as many ways to use social media as there are users of social media. Some people use it as a way to meet and to keep connected to others, whether in a personal capacity or a professional capacity or both. And for those who use it in these capacities, each individual will use it in their own way. Most people who use it for both personal and professional purposes will have multiple platforms for each purpose. For example, a service provider will most likely have a personal Facebook page for keeping connected with their family and friends but will also have a professional Facebook page for their professional services and information on their business. I keep both a personal page as well as a separate page for my law firm. On my personal page I try to post information and comments and share news stories that I find funny, important, and interesting to my audience—my family and friends. On my law firm's page, I post links to television spots that I have recently appeared on, upcoming or past events that my firm or I will be or have participated in such as speaking engagements, fundraisers, etc. I also post the services I offer, where my office is located, and any pertinent information regarding the courts and law that may affect my clients or prospective clients. Most importantly, I post multiple ways for people to contact me since that is the ultimate goal of using social media for professional purposes.

However, many people choose to use their social media platforms for very different purposes. During an election year, I saw that many people used their personal pages to post non-stop political statements, ads, and support for particular candidates, and even more so to post disparaging remarks and opinions of opposing candidates. I personally consider this to be a complete waste of time since I don't think anyone is interested in my political beliefs any more than I am interested in theirs, which is not at all. However, the magic of social media comes alive when people post potentially (whether intentionally or unintentionally) hot topics. That's when you really get to see what people are made of. Because anyone who can see your post, can also comment on it, which is why it's imperative for individuals and professionals to carefully think through each and every post they make on not only their own sites, but others' as well.

There are really two ways that social media can relate to probate litigation. Remember that most users are friends with family members on social media, and that most people have a chronic habit of posting about people they are with, places they have gone, and nice purchases they have made. And many people tend to forget that they truly are on a "world wide web." So in some cases, social media could be linked to causing litigation in that family members may see that other family members are spending money that they didn't use to have. Or that they are coming into possession of a deceased family member's personal property that they are not entitled to. It's not an unusual scenario that the use of social media would then cause a family member to pursue litigation because they believe or discover that the person settling an estate or trust is converting funds that they are not entitled to.

A more common scenario is that the family members are already embroiled in a controversy or litigation, and family members discover inconsistencies in the statements or claims. Let me give you a couple of examples.

In one case I studied, one of the fiduciary parties had paid a significant amount of estate money over to a gentleman who allegedly had worked with the decedent and taken care of the decedent prior to his death. At first this money was labeled as money due to a "caregiver." Of course that became problematic when it was pointed out by the beneficiaries' attorney that a caregiver can only be paid if there was a caregiver agreement in place. At that point the story changed. The story then became that the payee was actually a business partner with the decedent in a marijuana growing operation. But that became problematic because there were no records of this venture whatsoever. There was no income ever generated. There were no expenses ever claimed. There was no agreement between the parties as to how income and expenses were allocated, and of course, the "smoking gun," was that there were no marijuana plants!

Eventually, one of the beneficiaries did some research on Facebook and was able to download and print multiple vacation photos of the fiduciary and the "caregiver" on trips to tropical locations. Worse yet (for the fiduciary) were the captions that were included with the photos—clearly indicating that the man she claimed to be the dad's caregiver/business partner whom she had met a couple times was in fact her boyfriend.

So how was the beneficiary able to use the Facebook postings? Well, the posts were admissible as evidence in the same manner as any photograph and written statement. This not only proved to the court that the payments made to the caregiver/business partner were fraudulent, but it further exposed perjury on the part of the fiduciary since they had testified as to their relationship under oath. The parties never concluded the trial because the disclosure of the posts was enough to convince the parties to settle the case.

In another case I studied, the parties were unable to reach a resolution on how to divide their father's personal property left at his home, and how to divide or buy out the other party's share of the real estate that they inherited. The party in possession of the property kept reporting incidents of damage and theft of personal property on the premises. The other party staunchly denied it. This went on for over 18 months. Unfortunately, the spouse of one of the parties got sloppy and let their guard down and posted pictures and statements about the damage they had done over the weekend while removing personal property from the premises. Again, once the posts were shown to the other party's attorney, the disputes were resolved!

However, perhaps the most damaging effect of social media isn't necessarily the legal implications of our use of it in litigation. As you will see in the next section, the psychological effects of social media are deep, detrimental, and long-lasting.

The Psychological Effects of Social Media ("Cyberpsychology")

In most parts of the country, there has been an alarming increase in the number of teen/young adult suicides over the last decade. It crosses all socio-economic sectors, and all types of students. Every time I read about another young person lost to suicide it breaks my heart and starts me thinking again about what is causing this, for lack of a better word, pandemic. My son teaches high school at a local school so he and I were having a conversation about this. He made the comment that he believes that social media has played a large part in the increasing numbers. Again, being out of touch with both social media and teenagers, I really didn't buy that theory.

However, while obtaining my post-graduate certificate in forensic psychology, I was able to take an entire class on cyberpsychology and it was just the eye-opener I needed to understand that there is no doubt that social media has had and continues to have a profound impact on users' mental health. "Social media has a reinforcing nature. Using it activates the brain's reward center by releasing dopamine, a 'feel-good chemical' linked to pleasurable activities such as sex, food, and social interaction. The platforms are designed to be addictive and are associated with anxiety, depression, and even physical ailments." (McLean Hospital page 1) Therefore, you should always limit your social media usage, but particularly if and when you are feeling anxious, stressed, depressed, etc. And who hasn't been over the last 18 months? There are even physical manifestations of the stress it generates, such as nausea, headaches, muscle tension, and even tremors.

In addition to the physiological and physical responses that our bodies have to social media, the emotional fallout can be too much to bear with vulnerable persons, especially school-aged children. In addition to all the traditional bullying tactics that kids have always been subjected to, such as threats of being beaten up on the playground or after school, extortion of school lunch money, and "mean girl" phone calls to the home in the evening, cyber-harassment is becoming much too common. In other words, now the internet, and particularly social media, is a quick and easy way to mock, degrade, threaten, tease, and ostracize someone, with a literally unlimited audience! Add to that the fact that people will often make comments or posts online that they would not make in a face-to-face setting. This is called the "disinhibition effect," which refers to the lack of restraint a person feels when posting online as opposed to communicating face to face or in person. This is true also with telephone calls and text messages. People somehow feel safe and anonymous as if they are hidden behind their computer, phone, etc., even though their name is clearly shown as the source of the post. The obvious effect of this is that people fail to use their "filter" and end up posting much more negative comments and tend to use stronger language in their posts causing more bad feelings and stirring up additional negative postings by others on the site. This can create a snowball effect and be very detrimental to the target of the posts.

So for the litigants, social media can be a double-edged sword in that it can expose their nefarious actions, become evidence in a trial, expose fraud, perjury, and general mismanagement of assets or just damage their personal feelings of self-worth, embarrass them, and permanently damage their family relationships. While on the other hand, it can be a gold mine of evidence against the opposing party and be very valuable in either settling a lawsuit or winning at trial.

Social Media's Effects on Practicing Law

What about the effects of social media on attorneys? As I mentioned before, social media is a necessary evil that every attorney must manage and control to the extent possible. It's the opportunity to reach a large audience, to present their best face forward, and to create their own professional image. This is where the credentials and activities of the attorney can be spotlighted and where the attorney can develop rapport with potential and previous clients by engaging in dialogue. It's also a masterful educational tool where attorneys can post useful information and helpful tips, as well as posting instructional videos and on-demand seminars. The uses are limited only by the creativity and time allowances of the attorney.

Attorneys can close access to their social media sites, such as Facebook and websites, thereby preventing public postings to the site. However, many sites, such as LinkedIn, are designed to be interactive. Each post is set up for public comments and to be shared, as that is the goal of the site, to "spread the word" about the professional's accomplishments and contributions. However, those who either disagree with the posts or are disgruntled customers may also post their negative comments. And of course, anyone who has a social media account or profile, including with the likes of Twitter, YouTube, Tik Tok, Reddit, etc., can create any post they wish, including disparaging comments and critiques of the attorney. Even more disconcerting are the industry specific sites which are designed to rate the attorney. For example, in the legal profession there is a site called AVVO. I have found this site to be a double-edged sword: if you choose not to set up your profile on AVVO, its absence sends a negative message to those seeking your services, just like not having a website or a Facebook page. There are certain basic social media forums that are almost always searched and reviewed by potential clients. Google is kind enough to provide this format for you so all you have to do is update it (yes, you can hear the sarcasm in this sentence because I'm not a big fan of having a site automatically created on my behalf that literally anyone can post a review on without my knowledge). But in all seriousness, the lack of having a website or Facebook page or in my case an AVVO profile speaks louder than having one that isn't quite a 5-star site. And what social media giveth, social media can take away. The downside to AVVO is that others can post reviews that affect the attorney's rating.

It's critical to monitor each and every social media site on which you are potentially exposed to criticism and scathing reviews because human nature will cause the reader/researcher/potential client to weigh the negative comments and ratings more heavily than the positive ones. Ten positive comments and ratings can be undermined by just one scathing review—whether it's true or not! I have been put in the position of a former client who was disgruntled with their bill not only posting a very harmful review of me on social media, but also filing a grievance against me with the state Bar. Aside from the excruciating process of the grievance, the social media posting was very difficult to handle because the review cannot be removed by me! My only recourse was to have several other happy clients posts reviews so that the negative review would eventually get buried by the more recent reviews and the rating the client gave me would be averaged out with higher ratings. As a result of one disgruntled litigation client's review, it cost me a new estate planning client's business because they didn't feel they should work with me after reading her one review. I have also had another client literally threaten to post the most disparaging comments and ratings they could think of on any and all social media sites that they could find if I didn't write off their bill. And yes, they put this in writing! I felt like this was extortion but I wasn't going to push the issue over a modest out-standing balance. As a result I have increased my retainer amount so I don't get stuck writing off charges.

So what's the lawyer to do? Isn't this libel or slander? Yes, if the information is not true. However, opinion isn't fact, therefore, it's really not subject to being true or not true. Furthermore, the amount of money it would cost to litigate such a dispute would far exceed the amount that the client owes on their bill. Again, the best strategy is to limit the exposure to social media sites that allow public posting to them, and monitor them on a very regular, consistent basis. Why do I bring this subject up? The reason is two-fold. First, so that attorneys and other professionals can manage and control social media to their advantage to the extent possible, and second, to explain another outside influence and source of stress that attorneys need to be aware of and need to be prepared for. Having had a few unpleasant firsthand experiences,

I can say that it's extremely stressful to pour out your blood, sweat, and tears for someone else's family feud and then have to stand back and watch them undermine what you've worked so hard to build.

Conclusion

I think the impact of social media is just beginning to be understood on individuals and businesses, and certainly very few attorneys give much weight to its influence on their practice. I think that probate litigation in particular is affected more so than other areas of practice because of the fact that social media users are most likely related; therefore, the level of knowledge that the users have about each other and the emotional impact of communications on social media is heightened. In this chapter we have taken a brief look at how social media can and does impact relationships with family members, a user's psyche, how we try (and settle) lawsuits, and how it affects the way lawyers practice law. Stay tuned in this area. I think we will see much more research and reports on the long-term effects of social media on individuals, family members, and professionals.

References

McLean Hospital, "Like It Or Not, Social Media's Affecting Your Mental Health, November 4, 2020 (*McLean Hospital*)

CHAPTER 6:

LIFE AS A LITIGATOR:
WHO IS FIGHTING FOR YOU?

Introduction

For those of you attorneys who practice in any area of litigation, and for those of you non-attorneys, in this chapter we look at the darker side of practicing law, including attorney suicide, alcohol and substance abuse, depression, stress, and violence against attorneys. Many studies have been conducted and many articles and books have been written about these subjects and there isn't really an answer to the age-old question of which comes first, the chicken or the egg? In other words, are certain personality types and dispositions drawn to the legal profession, or does the legal profession cause these disorders? Regardless of which is the cause and which is the effect, this chapter looks at some raw statistics as well as situational factors that create some occupational hazards.

Hopefully, this chapter will also shed some light on what pro-active measures can be taken by the attorney to at least recognize and reduce stress and depression and their resulting alcohol and substance abuse and unfortunate suicides. We look at things like stress management, life management, and time management, which many lawyers struggle with. It seems that most lawyers feel like there just aren't enough hours in the day to do what they need to do, and having any kind of work/life balance is completely out of the question. As a Certified Personal Coach I hope I can help readers reclaim their turf, regardless of their occupation.

Alcohol & Substance Abuse and Suicide Among Attorneys

According to the CDC in 2013, lawyers ranked 4th in suicides when compared to other occupations. They are also 3.6 times more likely to suffer from depression than non-lawyers. And the suicides are on the rise. In fact, according to the article "Why Are Lawyers Killing Themselves?" (CNN.com/2014/01/19 ("CNN")), during 2004 the state of Oklahoma averaged one lawyer suicide per month; in South Carolina there were six lawyer suicides within 18 months before July of 2008; and there were 15 lawyer suicides in Kentucky between 2010 and 2014. The trend is so alarming that California, Montana, Iowa, Mississippi, Florida, South Carolina, and North Carolina all added a mental health component to mandatory Continuing Legal Education ("CLE") and Kentucky starts its annual conference on CLE with a presentation on behaviors that increase the risk of suicide (*CNN* at pages 2 and 3).

One attorney described his slow decline in mental health like this: after 27 years in the profession, he hit a wall, crashed, burned, and lost the one thing he always wanted to do, practice law. He was disciplined by the Oklahoma State Bar for failing to represent several clients. His clients demanded to know why he wasn't returning their calls. He began spending days in bed, locked in his home, hiding from his clients and his life. Sleep went from eight hours to six hours to four hours per night. He stopped engaging in any hobbies, stopped taking vacations, stopped socializing, and suffered through a divorce and loss of family. He believes that the profession is a magnet for workaholics who fall into a pattern where stress leads to depression, which can then trigger substance abuse or marital problems. Often disciplinary cases ensue (*CNN* at page 3 and 4).

Why is this happening? For one thing, in the legal profession, adversity is the nature of the game. Lawyers work in constant conflict: with other lawyers and opposing lawyers and insurance companies and judges and jurors and the Bar association. And even with their own clients on occasion. By its nature, the practice of law results in the lawyer shouldering the burden of the client's conflict and stress on behalf of the client. In probate litigation in particular, even though the lawyer is more detached from the conflict than the client (because the conflict doesn't involve the lawyer's family (in most situations anyway)), it still brings a unique form of stress to the attorney through their clients. However, that added stress and emotional burden on the client can create additional stress and emotional burden on the lawyer simply because the lawyer needs to deal with the client's emotional demands as well as the legal demands of the lawsuit. This can lead to conflict between the lawyer and the client, verbal abuse by the client against the lawyer, lack of cooperation on the part of the client, and failure of the client taking the lawyer's advice about the case. Quite often, the client becomes so emotionally involved that they can't make rational decisions about the case, particularly when it comes to any attempts of settlement negotiations and/or trial strategy. This is an indication that the client is out for revenge and therefore fails to focus on the reality of the legal position of the case. Eventually, the client will become so disenchanted that they do the one thing they can control; they stop paying the lawyer and refuse to settle up their final bill, adding more stress for the lawyer.

What can be done about it? Raising awareness and desensitizing the stigma of depression, suicide, and mental illness helps. Awareness of these issues has been increased largely by celebrities over the last 20–25 years. Suicides of such famous people as Robin Williams and Kate Spade have shown that mental illness is not just for the downtrodden and peripheral members of society. It's all around us, and many people, particularly celebrities, can hide it and become extremely successful even while dealing with it. This awareness and normalizing of mental illness helps others realize that they are not alone, and that they should not be embarrassed to admit that they are struggling and that they need help.

While the stigma is far from gone, I have seen a significant decrease in it just over my adulthood. For example, when I was growing up, it was not socially acceptable to "air your dirty laundry." In other words, you did not talk about negative issues that were going on in your family or household. This included any alcohol or substance abuse, poverty/job loss, emotional and/or physical abuse of the spouse and/or children, or any other stressors or traumas. There was little or no intervention on the part of the schools. While today there are mandatory reporting standards for teachers and counselors, there was no reporting when I was growing up. In fact, it would have been categorically rejected if any school personnel tried to discuss or intervene in any personal issues in the home or family. When I look back, I can name a few classmates that everyone knew were being physically abused, yet nobody did anything about it. And because there was no discussion about such issues, there was correspondingly no discussion about the emotional effect of these issues, let alone any treatment programs available. And parents certainly didn't want to admit that their children had any emotional or cognitive issues because it was looked at as a parental failure. It was a vicious cycle that resulted in many damaged adults who often lack relationship skills.

Fortunately, now the schools and physicians and social services organizations are trained and encouraged and required to be screening for such problems, and there are multiple avenues for mental health and cognitive deficiency treatments. While funding isn't as healthy as it could be, it is leaps and bounds ahead of where we were even 30 years ago.

Another exciting breakthrough in mental health includes the ability to monitor the brain activity and chemical responses in the body to mental illness and treatments. Under the topic, *Stress and Arousal: The Flight or Fight Response* (pages 178–180 in "Abnormal Psychology" by Comer) we see that multiple body systems are activated during stress and arousal: the autonomic nervous system, the endocrine system, and the sympathetic nervous system, causing physical, emotional, and cognitive responses in the body. By understanding what is going on in the body and brain, we can now better create treatments for mental illness, whether that's through medicines, therapies, counseling, neurofeedback, or a combination of them. The fact that these illnesses have physiological causes and effects also helps de-stigmatize them. For some reason, people find dealing with physical ailments and diseases socially acceptable but are embarrassed by psychological or mental ailments.

In addition to social stigmatization, the other factor that often prevents lawyers from getting help for depression and stress management is a lack of funding. Many lawyers are self-employed and do not have comprehensive health plans. Even with employer-provided health insurance, mental health treatment is not typically paid at the same rate as physical health services. Many state Bars, including Michigan's, offer free treatment for alcohol and substance treatment for members and their families, but they refer out treatment for depression and mental health issues that don't include alcohol and substance abuse. That takes the lawyer back to funding issues. Personally, I've always thought it would make more sense to offer free treatment for the depression and anxiety before the substance abuse becomes a problem, but not everyone agrees with that approach.

Lawyers who practice in large firms by and large don't have the stress of the everyday practice management of the firm, meaning, they don't have to spend time and energy running a business. While the stresses of running a business are removed from their plate, that doesn't mean that they don't have stressors that solo or small firm lawyers have. In lieu of the practice management tasks, they take on the stressors of being part of a corporate environment. They have to meet the demands of the partners of the firm in terms of billable hours, rainmaking, company politics and policies, and public persona. Anyone who has worked in a corporate environment or watched the movie "Office Space" can understand the stressors of working for other people and the expectations of the company's management. Further, the expectations of the upper echelon (i.e., partners), is that every lawyer plans on working their way up to partner level, which brings additional stressors for the lawyers to perform and produce.

Regardless of what size firm the lawyer is practicing in, client management can be one of the largest sources of stress, particularly in probate litigation. One question that every law student is taught to ask themselves is, "Who is the client?" In most lawsuits the answer to that is obvious. In civil litigation you have plaintiffs and defendants, typically one individual versus another individual or versus an insurance company. In family law, the lawyer represents either one spouse or the other, or one parent or the other, and so on. However, in probate litigation, the answer to this question can become much more difficult to answer. Why? Because the person who hires you must be an affected party in the lawsuit (i.e., must be one of the interested parties covered in Michigan Court Rules of 1985 rule number 5.125), but that doesn't mean they are the one calling the shots. In addition, they may be the only family member who is willing or able to step up and bring the lawsuit, but they may actually be "ghost representing" for lack of a better word, other family members. For example, family disputes usually result in certain family members forming "sides," like a gang. One family member may actually hire the lawyer and be the named party on the court filings, but they may just be the designated leader of multiple family members who are making decisions and calling the shots behind the scenes. Sometimes I look at the family member who hires the lawyer as the sacrificial lamb because the others are throwing them out to take the heat of the lawsuit while they all sit back and give direction and opinion without the help of the lawyer. By far the worst scenarios I have worked with involve the client's spouses being the driving force behind litigation. It's not unusual for the spouses of the family members to be the most forceful and emotionally driven persons in the group. These sacrificial lamb scenarios can be by far the most difficult clients to work with. Here's why:

Most family members who are engaged in litigation with each other have some innate sense of family alliance in spite of the pending litigation. They have an underlying emotional conflict because as angry and hurt as they may feel towards the opposing family member(s), they also have the underlying love and connection that pulls them back. They also recognize that there are two sides to everything, and they know all the skeletons in the closet. And since the majority of feuding families are a result of alcohol/substance abuse, abuse and/or neglect by the parents, blended family situations, etc., they strangely have a bond that outsiders don't share. They've been through the same hell. This is what makes probate litigation so emotionally painful and stressful to the parties. I often have non-litigation clients remark to me that they cannot imagine being in a lawsuit against their own family members. They repeatedly say things like, "But it's your *family*," or "How could you do that to your own family members?" So, while the litigating family members are carrying deep feelings of anger, resentment, hurt, distrust, and pain, they also have the unique bond that outsiders just can't understand. In some respects, they have compassion for the opposing parties.

Contrast that with the position that the litigating family members' spouses are in. They have no childhood history or common bond with the parties. They may have a history with them as an in-law, but they don't share that common bond of being siblings or step-siblings, or whatever familial relationship there is. They didn't go through the trenches with these people as children and they quite often don't even know what dysfunction the family members may have endured. Much of it is unspoken. From the spouse's perspective, they are more able to detach themselves from the compassion (usually they have none for the opposing party anyway), and the emotional bond, and they definitely do not see any other side to the story. What they do see is the amount of pain and suffering that their spouse has endured and is enduring. For those reasons, they are more likely to be out for revenge and can be much more cold and calculating.

It's also important to recognize when the family member/ client is being subject to the spouse's undue influence, bullying, and sometimes outright emotional abuse. Because of my training as a Domestic Relations Mediator, which requires an additional eight-hour training on domestic violence screening, I am always looking for signs of potential emotional and/or physical spousal abuse. For example, is the client in direct communication with the lawyer or is the client's spouse? Is the client deferring to the spouse when it comes to decision making on the case? And is the client always accompanied by or including the spouse in telephone calls, zoom calls or in person meetings? These can be signs of abuse.

What should you look for? Look at who contacted the lawyer. Was it the family member or the spouse? If it was the spouse, why did the spouse contact the lawyer instead of the family member? Sometimes it's simply a matter of logistics, such as the family member has a job that doesn't lend itself to communicating with the lawyer as efficiently. Or maybe the spouse knows the lawyer so they reach out to make the initial connection. But sometimes it's a warning sign of who is really driving the train.

During the litigation process, who is the one that reaches out to the lawyer, has calls and strategy sessions with the lawyer, and provides the documentation and evidence to the lawyer? Again, this may be another matter of logistics. However, you should be concerned if this is a regular pattern, and the actual family member/client is sitting quietly during meetings and calls, or worse yet, isn't really engaged at all. If you're the lawyer, test the waters by trying to have an isolated meeting or conversation alone with the family member client. If this is met with obstruction, rejection, or any other difficulty, you have a problem and it needs to be dealt with immediately. In severe situations, that may even mean that you need to withdraw from representation.

So outside forces play a significant role in probate litigation and particularly settlement opportunities. Because of the emotional attachment between the family members, the parties will feel the emotional stress of litigation much more quickly and more intensely than the outsiders will. They are typically more agreeable to a settlement than the outsiders because they are ready for it to end so they can get their life back and move forward. The outsiders will have much more stamina to keep litigating and often will not be happy until they get their pound of flesh. Make no mistake, all of this emotional baggage and difficult client management will eventually bleed over to the lawyer. That's why recognizing and understanding what's going on is so critical for the lawyer, and the earlier the better.

How do you handle these situations? Well, sadly, I've learned the hard way, by trial and error. Again, recognizing the situation early on is key. Set those boundaries and rules of engagement early in the relationship. Make it clear that in order to do your job well, and in order to comply with ethics rules on confidentiality and representation, you *must* have an independent consultation and candid meeting with the actual client. Don't be shy about discussing the attorney-client relationship, the ethics requirements, and why it's important to handle the case that way. The trick is to do this without insulting the outsider and without getting fired. You want to emphasize that keeping the lines of communication open is important and if the client wants the outsider to talk with the lawyer or provide documents to the lawyer, that's fine, but do whatever you need to do to *make sure the client feels free to express how they really feel to the lawyer!* In any kind of abusive relationship, that's going to be a challenge. Abusers don't really like anyone isolating the victim because they are afraid of what the victim is going to say. And possibly, they don't have any confidence in the victim's decision making.

Which leads me to another potential issue: the capacity of the client. Mental or cognitive capacity is a very common issue in probate proceedings in some way shape or form. If you notice that the outsider is the one doing all the talking, or making decisions for the client and otherwise inserting themselves into the conflict, you should make sure that the underlying problem isn't that the outsider is using the family member as a pawn to get standing to litigate. For example, if the affected family member is an elderly parent and it's a contested guardianship or conservatorship case, is the adult child the one bringing in the parent and doing all the talking? How aware is the actual client of the proceedings and the issues at hand? And how much do they really care about the issues? If in doubt, don't be afraid to isolate the client to make an armchair assessment of their capacity. And if you're still in doubt, don't be afraid to recommend having a psychological assessment done on them. If a client lacks capacity to enter into a contract, they also lack the capacity to engage your services. And they also lack the capacity to participate in the litigation. You need to determine that at the outset of representation and not during trial.

Although it's an oversimplification, most lawyers are stressed by two main stressors: not enough time to get the work done, and, carrying the emotional baggage of the clients. I believe that getting some solid time management programs in place is the first step. If you can control your time, you can control much of your stress.

Time management (as well as money management) is really an exercise in priorities. We are all given a finite amount of time and money (i.e. resources). How a person allocates these two resources in their personal and professional lives is a direct function of their priorities. For example, you may often hear a friend or neighbor say that they don't have time to attend a certain function, or mow their lawn or whatever the case may be, yet the next thing you know they are going to sporting events, out for dinner with their friends, and taking a vacation four times a year. Clearly, they have the same 24 hours in the day, 7 days in the week, and 365 days in the year that you have. So, if they have time to go to dinner, take vacations, and attend sporting events, they *could* attend social events or mow their lawn. What they really mean is that they are choosing to spend their finite amount of time attending sporting events, going out for dinner with friends, and taking multiple vacations *rather than* tending to the items that they claim they don't have time for. This is simply an allocation of resources. This theory is even more evident when it comes to spending money. How many people do you know who say they can't afford something (fill in the blank here, it could be a car, a vacation, a new house, clothes, the list goes on forever), and yet they find the money to buy a new RV, a motorcycle, a timeshare (again, the list goes on forever). This is a direct allocation of their resources. People allocate resources according to their priorities whether they realize it or not.

Why do I bring this up? Because as an attorney, time is money, and time is limited. Most professionals I know feel stressed from their work because they feel that there is not enough time to complete their work. The word "overwhelmed" is used a lot. And for lawyers, too much work is a good problem to have because, again, time is money, and too little work means no revenue. In addition, most overwhelmed professionals feel that their time is out of their control, and to a large extent, it can be. Being in a service industry, it's important to make sure to take phone calls when the phone rings, respond to emails when it hits the inbox, etc. So when do you have time to actually do the work? This is where early mornings, late nights, and weekends in the office become habit. I propose that the busy professional start by aligning their priorities with their calendar.

Yes, easier said than done; however, that doesn't mean you can't make a significant difference in the stress levels with your job and your life. When working as a personal coach, I start by using what some coaches call, "Wheel of Life" forms. We simply draw a circle and draw lines as if you're cutting a pie. Then we either make a copy of that one or draw another so that we have two. One is for your work life and one is for you overall work and personal life. Then these wheels are divided into eight sections, each section representing one aspect of life. For the personal wheel, we use topics such as career, family and friends, significant others/romance, physical environment, fun and recreation, personal growth, money, and health. For the professional wheel we use topics such as time management, success in working with others, career, coaching, work/life balance and well-being, relationship(s) with management and team members, results, and any other topic that is important to the client. The goal is to think about each section and rate it in terms of how satisfied you are with that segment of your work or overall life, then shade in the wheel from the center to that line. Once you have completed each section, observe the wheel as if it were a tire on your car. How much air is in your tires? How smooth is the ride in your car? I recommend starting with the "flattest" spot on your tire and making some changes. Once you increase your level of satisfaction in one segment to an acceptable level, move on to another segment until your tires are "properly inflated" and your life is a "smooth ride" (to the extent that it can be). Once you start making improvements in one segment, you will most likely find that other segments have naturally increased in your satisfaction as well. This is particularly true if you have been feeling overwhelmed or significantly dissatisfied with your work life.

So, how do you take back control of your work life and specifically your calendar? There is no one particular method or product(s) that is unequivocally *the* way to go. Just like there are no absolute weight loss methods that are the *best*. Each person has to find a program and/or product(s) that match their priorities and their lifestyle. But a few rules of thumb can be applied to every individual in finding what method(s) work best for you.

For attorneys, a change in mindset is critical. I have an attorney friend who literally blocks off times during her workday to read and respond to emails, and notes that in her automatic response email. What a brilliant idea! The point is that you *don't* have to respond to every call or every email at that particular moment. Once you have established a schedule that works for you, plan your work and work your plan. If you block off an hour to address emails and return phone calls, then ignore them until that time. By the way, not only is this much better for *you*, but it's also better for your *clients* because whether you are working on a brief or responding to an email, your focus at that moment is on that particular client's needs. No more stopping your legal argument in a Motion for Summary Disposition to take a quick phone call or respond to an email about whether a client can access grandmother's personal property in her house that afternoon.

There are more time management and calendaring programs out there than anyone can count. In my case, I use multiple systems, both electronic and handwritten. It takes a little longer to make sure they are all synchronized, but going through the process is part of managing my time. You may find that using one system for your overall day, which could include personal and professional commitments, and another system for your workday works best for you. Here is an example of a two-schedule approach:

Overall Day Monday through Friday:

5:30 am – 7:00 am: Wake up, get showered and fed and ready for work. Leave for work.

7:00 am – 5:00 pm: Work activities.

5:00 pm -6:30 pm: Travel home, walk the dog, eat dinner.

7:00 pm -8:30 pm: Bible study/board meetings/
catch up on reading/etc.

8:30 pm – 10:00 pm: Organize for the next day,
relax, hobbies, etc.

10:00 pm -5:30 am: Sleep.

Workday:

7:00 am – 8:00 am: review and respond to emails, review
calendar for the day, marketing, other administrative tasks.

8:00 am – 9:00 am: Writing block/drafting block.

9:00 am – 12:30 pm: Various casework tasks, such as
client meetings, phone calls, hearings, depositions, etc.

12:30 pm – 1:00 pm: Lunch.

1:00pm – 2:30 pm: Read and respond to emails;
return phone calls.

2:30 pm – 4:00 pm: Client meetings, drafting
and research time, etc.

4:00 pm – 5:00 pm: Review caseload and make list of upcoming
tasks and list in order of priority; follow up on any other time-
sensitive matters, connect with clients who have hearings the
next day, etc.

So, the work calendar is really a subset of the overall life
calendar.

Obviously, this is just one example and it will change each day depending on court hearings, discovery dates, etc. You may also want to add in a weekly staff meeting or other non-billable work. The point is, by sitting down and planning your day and working your plan to the extent possible, you will feel much more in control of your time (and life) because you *will be* much more in control of your time. One thing is true about time and money—either you manage it or it manages you. It won't be perfect by any means, but the more you plan and the more you work your plan, the more in control you will be, the better quality you will be able to deliver to your clients, and the healthier and happier you will be. You can anticipate some pushback from others until you show them that you are serious about sticking to your plan and that it does work. It takes some time to get used to ignoring emails and calls until a designated time, and it will take some time for your staff not to interrupt you if you're in a designated work block, but stick with it—it will pay off.

Journaling is also a tried and true method of stress management. Journaling is recommended in literally every self-help program from weight loss, to time management, to financial management. Journaling on a regular basis, preferably daily, can help you set goals, record your thoughts and concerns, track what you did/spent/ate, and pour out your thoughts without judgment. It's helpful to record something you are grateful for that day, no matter how insignificant it might seem, and to record something that you would like to do better or improve upon the next day. By reviewing your journals, you can track patterns of behavior that might not be working, and conversely, see the trend of what's improving. If you're concerned about others finding your journal, you can always tear out the sheets and burn them—just the act of writing it down has its own benefits.

You will see that I did not include a particular time slot to go to the gym or workout. I recognize that food intake and physical exertion are a critical part of your overall physical and mental health regime. However, each person can prioritize those habits in their own schedule. For me, I walk the dog at least three times a week, and then try to do something more strenuous like kayaking or biking on the weekends. Whatever works for you works for you.

Other self-care practices might be massage therapy, getaway weekends, diet modifications such as eliminating sugars, fats, and alcohol and focusing on lean proteins and fresh fruits and vegetables, and making a commitment to attend social functions such as concerts, sporting events, and working on hobbies. Just make sure that you are addressing your physical and mental requirements, and do what works for you. There is no right or wrong.

Violence Against Attorneys (By Clients and/or Opposing Parties)

As if lawyers aren't self-destructive enough, violence against attorneys is not all that unheard of. Judges and prosecutors are often threatened not only by litigants, but also by family members, friends, and gang members of defendants. While criminal defense attorneys may gain favor from clients and their associates they don't often gain favor from the victims. And civil cases are not immune from violence against attorneys, either. Family law cases such as divorce and child custody disputes and certainly probate litigation issues are highly emotional cases and for many people the stakes are quite high. Add in the fact that many of the parties are or have been victims of some type of abuse and you have the firepower for a party to reach their limit and try to take it out on an attorney.

I can remember hearing about lawyers being shot and killed by clients and opposing parties all the way back in my childhood. I even know of one person whose divorce lawyer had an attempted car bombing from the opposing party in the last 15 years. With violent crimes in general becoming more common, it's even more important for lawyers to think about protecting themselves. Therefore, having an enhanced perception of human emotion and precognitive awareness will contribute towards preventative actions.

There are really two different times that you need to consider protecting yourself. One is when you are out in public, particularly when you will be attending a court hearing or trial, and the other is when you are working at your office. Obviously, you have much less control over your safety when you are out in public; however, security in and around courthouses has been increased substantially even within the last 10 years.

Whether or not you feel the need or feel comfortable carrying a weapon is a personal decision and beyond the scope of this book. However, whether you are carrying a weapon or not, you must be aware of your surroundings at all times. Park as close to the courthouse as possible and in a high traffic, well-lit area whenever possible. Wear "smart" shoes so that you can move quickly and with agility if necessary. For those of you who grew up with "Charlie's Angels," have you ever actually tried to run and pivot and jump with three-inch heels on? I would say go ahead and try it but I don't want any lawsuits when it ends in an emergency room visit. Once you are in the courthouse, you are probably the safest from gunfire (or from a hatchet, such as the one a woman tried to bring into a nearby courthouse that I practiced in) because literally all the courthouses I have entered within the last 10 years have security and metal detectors. However, that doesn't mean you are protected from any kind of "manual" violence such as getting beaten up. At a minimum, you will most likely be subjected to verbal abuse. For these reasons, I highly recommend that you do not take the elevator with opposing parties or their witnesses. I don't particularly recommend that you take the stairs either since you could get confronted in the stairwell. Just wait for your own elevator. If you feel threatened getting back to your vehicle, you may ask the court to have a deputy escort you to your car. I actually had a judge ask a deputy to escort me to my car when she heard the opposing party making threats to me while we were still in the courtroom.

When working in your office, you should have a security plan in place. This should be in writing and should be shared with your staff as well. You can even make it part of the employee handbook. Some of the items you may want to include in your plan could be

- Keeping the doors to your office suite locked

- Screening your staff with criminal background checks

- Training your employees in the security plan

- Control access to your building as well as your suite to the extent that this is within your control

- If you own the building, consider installing security cameras and an alarm system

- Be observant of people entering and exiting the parking lot, building, and offices

- Obtain a list of local crimes online at www.crimemapping.com

- Develop lockdown areas and an evacuation plan

- Remember the three-step analysis in the event of an active shooter: Run! Hide! Fight! Running is the best option, hiding is the second best option, and fighting is the third option.

- See something? Hear something? *Say* something.

- Deal with disruptive individuals calmly and assertively, but be polite and professional

- Ask the person to leave the building.
  If they don't, call 9-1-1

- Preferably use a key or swiped card entrance
  that locks automatically when closed

- Have well-lit parking areas, preferably close to the doors

- Also include security plans for fires, bomb threats,
  tornadoes, and earthquakes (yes, we have earthquakes
  in Michigan every now and then, too!)

- Conduct a risk assessment of your building and office

- You may consider showing the YouTube video Run/Hide/
  Fight as part of your employee on-boarding process

- Make staff aware of potential threats such as current or
  previous clients, opposing parties, opposing counsel,
  patrons, and tenants in the building

- Identify "safe areas" such as interior rooms and closets,
  behind filing cabinets, bathrooms if they lock, etc.

- Identify escape routes such as windows and alternate doors,
  and even other suites in the building

- Keep a piece of "door blocking" furniture near the door

- Keep a stocked first aid kit in the office

- Create email and text notifications to all staff and attorneys

- Offer post-event counseling for any employees involved in a workplace security event

- Review the Homeland Security Emergency Action Plan Guide Active Shooter Awareness available online

Each security plan will be different depending on the office location, type of building, etc. While no plan is fail-safe, no plan is also no plan.

Conclusion

This chapter should help the reader understand the significance of stress that lawyers face as part of their job. Not too long ago, lawyers were highly respected professionals and leaders of the community. To some extent they were placed upon a pedestal and highly regarded and rarely questioned. They were treated much more like physicians, as helpers rather than hindrances, protagonists rather than antagonists. They were also some of the wealthiest folks in town. Yes, things have definitely changed!

No longer are lawyers treated as kindly as they were. It's important to understand that practicing law is a demanding and often draining profession. Hopefully this chapter has helped the reader understand why that is and how the negative aspects of the profession can be minimized, along with the emotional and physical effects of the stress associated with it. Prevention is so important, whether its prevention of alcohol and substance abuse, professional burnout, or violence against lawyers, taking time to think, plan, and follow through can produce significant results. And if nothing else, I hope that the reader is more inclined to seek professional help if they find themselves struggling.

References

Abnormal Psychology by Ronald J. Comer, 9th Edition (*Abnormal Psychology, 9th edition by Comer*)

CNN.com/2014/01/19 *(CNN)*

CHAPTER 7:

CONCLUSION

So, what can we take away from this book? Depending on whether you are an attorney or non-attorney will obviously affect what you have learned or found interesting in this book. My hope is that regardless of your reasons for reading it, you will have at least come away with the following points.

First, families are taking each other to court to challenge a will or trust or the actions of a family member's actions while serving as a fiduciary in increased numbers. The reasons for this are many as we have seen. Many are due to an underlining mental illness either in a parent or one of the siblings. Add to that the fact that many of those who suffer from mental illness are undiagnosed and/or improperly treated, leaving them to self-treat with alcohol or other substance use. Trauma in the family, whether from emotional, sexual, or physical abuse or more likely some combination thereof can be buried for years and the results of which may not surface for decades until the parents have passed away. We also see that situational factors play a role in driving these cases, such as blended families, family businesses, or simply a lack of proper planning. Another theory I have but is not necessarily one that parties will ever admit is the fact that for many middle aged adults, the inheritance they expect to receive from their parents is in fact their retirement. Previous generations lived within their means, tended to avoid consumer credit, and were savers. Often times they were products of the great depression and always feared running out of money. They bought modest houses, paid them off in full, and lived there most of their adult lives. Therefore, when they passed away, there was little debt to pay off and typically at least a modest amount of assets to distribute. Contrast that with their children's generation who are now middle-aged and have lived in an unprecedented era of consumer credit and government programs so that most people do not have to fear providing for their basic needs of food, clothing and shelter. In fact, most middle-aged adults have enjoyed years of conspicuous consumption by taking advantage of consumer credit and effectively living above their means. As a result, they tend not to be savers. This combination of circumstances can create a powerful incentive for siblings to fight to maximize their inheritance because it may just be the only funds they have for their retirement years.

The result of this trend in litigation is that more and more families are undergoing the financial and emotional destruction of their relationships and ending up in much worse shape than they expected. Hopefully one take away from this book is that proper planning, regardless of whether you believe your family will end up in court, is more important than ever.

Another take away from this book is a better understanding of how the legal process of litigation works, specifically in contested probate matters. If you're a Michigander, you can better understand the laws and court rules that drive the process and ultimately determine the outcome of your case. Armed with this information, you should have a more realistic expectation if you are contemplating or involuntarily embroiled in such proceedings.

Some readers may feel that this book drifts over into irrelevant information regarding the history of mental illness as well as a primer in common mental disorders. However, to me, those subjects are really the key to what drives family discord. We now live in a very enlightened society when it comes to recognizing, understanding, treating and discussing mental illness. And we still have a very long way to go. But when you compare where we are now with where society was when our middle-aged population was growing up, you can see that we are just now realizing and recognizing the impact of what was going on inside the family units and the results decades later. So by having a better understanding of the psychology and social history we can better deal with current family disputes and hopefully avoid many such disputes in the future.

Apart from the psychological forces that drive these cases, the situational causes are equally important. As divorce rates began skyrocketing in the 1970's and have now become the unfortunate "normal" in families (if the parents ever married at all), the blended family has become commonplace. Add to that the fact that we have transitioned to the majority of families living off two incomes instead of one. This means that both parents, whether still married at their death or not, may have substantial assets upon their death particularly if they participated in a retirement plan during their working years. And a third factor we commonly see now is that if the first spouse dies even in their 60's, the surviving spouse is likely to remarry and have a 20+ year subsequent marriage. Are you in one of these situations? Are your parents in one of these situations? If so, I hope that you have learned the importance of proper planning so that your family does not end up in court fighting over assets, or equally disturbing, accidentally left out because of improper planning. As was discussed earlier, other situational factors can lead to litigation but the key take away is that these situational factors don't have to lead the family to court because they can all be properly planned for.

Whether you're a lawyer or non-lawyer you have been and will continue to be affected by social media. For the lawyers reading this, I hope you have a better understanding of how to manage social media to your advantage and minimize the damage it can do to your career and your practice. If you're a non-lawyer, I hope that you have a better understanding of two things. First, social media can be a treasure trove of evidence in family conflicts for the lawyers, so be extremely careful what you post online as well as what you email and text to others. Second, if you find yourself hiring a layer for any reason, I hope you think twice about the impact that your comments and reviews can have on their reputation and practices. While it might feel good at the time to "warn" others about the hack job you believe the lawyer performed for you on your case, there are always two sides to everything and once you post something online, it's not going away. Think about how you would feel if someone made comments and rankings to your employer based on their perception of how you did your job. It's always best to try to have a conversation with the attorney to express your concerns and disappointments directly with them.

Another section of this book probably seemed out of place to many readers. I'm referring to the chapter on self-help. That chapter was definitely aimed at the lawyers reading the book because I think it's important for them to know that they are not alone in the pressure and stress that they feel from practicing in this area of law, or in any litigation matters. But the same principles apply to the non-lawyer readers. We all face an internal tug-of-war between all the many roles we play: employee, spouse, parent, grand-parent, neighbor, volunteer, etc. And very job has its own form of stress. If the job was easy and fun all the time, they wouldn't pay you to do it. So hopefully all readers can take away some tips on stress management, safety and overall well-being.

And finally, I hope that this book was both educational as well as enjoyable to read. Whether or not you are an attorney, you should come away with much more knowledge about this area of the law as well as some good stories! Thank you for taking the time to read this!